W9-BXX-543

DON'T FORGET YOUR FREE BOOKS

THE GREAT BOOK OF FOOTBALL

Interesting Facts and Sports Stories

Sports Trivia Vol.2

Bill O'Neill
&
Ryan Black

CONTENTS

INTRODUCTION

If you love the NFL, you've got the perfect book in your hands. This is a celebration of American football played at its highest form—in the National Football League. From Gale Sayers and George Halas to Tom Brady and Bill Belichick, the NFL has never lacked for characters, championships, courage, or controversy. Through it all, the passion and love felt by the hands for this uniquely American game have endured and propelled the league higher and higher in terms of popularity and world recognition.

Of course, telling all those stories would take a lifetime to research, a decade to write, and a year or two to read! In this edition, we've taken some of the greatest stories from across the nearly 100-year history of the NFL and presented them in digestible form, spread across seven chapters that span the league's history.

There are ten stories per chapter along with fifteen astonishing facts, figures, and statistics that you'll have to read to believe, along with five trivia questions that will test your mettle as an NFL fan and let you in turn stump your football-loving friends next time you get together to watch a game.

Whether it's the morning of the Super Bowl or the middle of the offseason, this book is the perfect pigskin companion for any avid football fan. Let's kick it off!

CHAPTER 1

BIRTH OF A LEAGUE

The early days of the NFL make it rather amazing that the league has lasted so long. There were ten teams in four states, everyone wore a leather helmet they could fold up and put in their pocket, and franchises with names like the Muncie Flyers and Toledo Maroons actually existed.

Humble Beginnings

If you've never heard of the Hupmobile, you're not alone. This brand of automobile started up in 1909 and had vanished from the marketplace by World War II. Yet it was at a Hupmobile dealership in a little town called Canton, Ohio, that the NFL was originally brought together. It was only the teams of the Ohio League that first day as the American Professional Football Conference was formed. A month later, the league was renamed the American Professional Football Association, with Buffalo, Rochester, Detroit, and Hammond coming in along with a few others. The original eleven franchises put together a charter saying they would not steal players from one another (a practice called poaching back in the day), and they would declare an end-of-season champion.

The first league president was American legend Jim Thorpe, who was also still an active player at the time. The first season, in 1920, was full of scheduling flaws and stumbling blocks, and only four of the eleven teams finished their seasons entirely, with the Akron Pros named league champions. The following year, membership doubled to 22 teams, with most of the newcomers hailing from New York State. Just two teams from that original year are still in the league. The Decatur Staleys eventually became the Chicago Bears, while the Chicago Cardinals eventually moved to St. Louis and then out west to Arizona. While baseball struggled with allowing black players into the late 1940s, the NFL originally allowed them to play, but stopped that practice in 1927, going nearly twenty years before reintegrating. The league had been close to forming twice before in the 1910s. The first time, it was cut short by the US' entry into World War I. The second time, a flu pandemic that began in 1918 and killed 3-5 percent of the world's population limited travel of teams, as 28% of the US contracted the disease, and a horrifying estimate of between 500,000-675,000 died.

Jim Thorpe

If Jim Thorpe were a young man today, he would have 500 million followers on Twitter, make $500 million a year in endorsements, and have a 24-hour news channel dedicated solely to his every move. Thorpe was the great American athlete in the time before

Babe Ruth started slamming home runs every other day. A member of the Sac and Fox Nation, he was born in 1887 in what is now Oklahoma. In 1904, at age 16, Thorpe went to Carlisle Indian Industrial School and was coached by none other than Glenn Scobey "Pop" Warner. He competed in football, baseball, lacrosse, and everyone's favorite sport, ballroom dancing, in which he won the 1912 intercollegiate championship. Ironically, Warner didn't want him playing football because he was so incredible on the track. At Carlisle College, he played running back, defensive back, placekicker, and punter, and scored all his team's points in an 18-15 upset win of No. 1 Harvard.

In 1912, Carlisle won the national title as Thorpe rushed for 1,869 yards on just 191 carries, scoring 25 touchdowns. He also competed in the 1912 Summer Olympics in the decathlon and pentathlon, winning gold in both events and winning eight of the fifteen competitions outright. He went on to play a smattering of seasons of Major League Baseball with the New York Giants, Cincinnati Reds, and Boston Braves over the next few years, but also went back to his first love of football. He signed with the Canton Bulldogs in 1915 for the large sum of $250 per game, and the team's attendance rose from 1,200 to 8,000 per game. Canton won the league title in 1916, 1917, and 1919, and joined the APFA in 1920 with Thorpe as president. He played until age 41, having racked up 52 NFL games for six teams from 1920-1928.

Green Bay Packers

There had been a semipro team in Green Bay, Wisconsin, as early as 1896, and Earl Lambeau and George Calhoun were determined to follow suit in the late 1910s. Lambeau and Calhoun had been rivals on the high school football field but now teamed up to make something special happen. Lambeau had been the captain of Green Bay East High School's football team and its captain in 1917. In 1918, he played for Knute Rockne at Notre Dame. The team formed in 1919, didn't field a team in 1920, then joined the newly formed NFL on August 27, 1921. They've played in the NFL every year since, the longest consecutive franchise in the league. Within their first decade on the field, the Packers became the class of the league. In 1927, they went 7-2-1 under Lambeau's leadership as a player and coach. Only the New York Giants (11-1-1) were better.

They went 12-0-1 in 1929, shutting out eight of their thirteen opponents. For the entire season, they allowed just 22 points—three touchdowns and a pair of safeties. In their showdown with perennial power New York, they trounced the Giants 20-6.

They repeated as league champions in 1930 and 1931, with their first crop of Hall of Famers like Mike Michalske, Johnny McNally, Carl Hubbard, and folk hero Arnie Herber, a Green Bay native. During that first heyday, the Packers won 29 straight home games, a record that has never been broken. They ended the year with three straight shutouts, and a crowd of 20,000 fans greeted them when they blasted their biggest rival, the Chicago Bears, 25-0 to end the season.

They went 10-3-1 in 1930, finishing mere percentage points ahead of the Giants (13-4) for the title. They split their season series with New York, winning 14-7 at home and losing 13-6 on the road. In 1931, the Packers became the first team to win three NFL titles in a row when they finished the season with a 12-2 record. This time, their closest rival was the Portsmouth Spartans, who went 11-3. In all, the Packers would win eleven titles between 1929-1967 and have added four Super Bowl wins since.

The 1925 Title Dispute

Just six seasons into the formation of the NFL, the league suffered it first controversy. Five new teams had entered the league—the New York Giants, the Detroit Panthers, the Providence Steam Roller, the new Canton Bulldogs, and the Pottsville Maroons.

The Maroons were an instant success, winning six of their first seven games, all by shutout. Their only loss was to the Providence Steam Roller by a 6-0 margin. The rest of their games they won by a combined score of 179-0.

Their biggest game of the season came on December 6, when they knocked off the Chicago Cardinals 21-7 on the road. The victory should have given Pottsville the NFL title, but the following week they scheduled a game to play the University of Notre Dame All-Stars in Philadelphia, winning 9-7. The Frankford Yellow Jackets played a game the same day in Philadelphia and complained to the league that Pottsville had violated its territorial rights. NFL president Joe Carr fined the club and then suspended it from all league rights and privileges, including the right to play for the championship. The Cardinals went on to play two more games and wound up 11-2-1 with the Maroons at 10-2-0. In 2003, the NFL put to its owners the idea of reopening the case, but the league voted 30-2 against it, with only Pottsville and fellow Pennsylvania franchises, the Steelers and Eagles voting in favor.

George Halas

Halas was always a lucky one, starting in 1915 when he was running late and missed boarding the SS Eastland, which went on to capsize and kill all 844 passengers. He was a cofounder of the NFL and retired with the nickname "Mr. Everything." Small wonder, he founded and owned the Chicago Bears, played in the league, was a radio producer, an inventor, and even a professional baseball player. He went to the University of Illinois and played baseball, basketball, and football for the Illini, earning a degree in civil engineering in his spare time and helping the football team win the 1918 Big Ten Conference title. He would have gone straight to pro after football but instead was an ensign in the Navy during World War I where he played for the Great Lakes Naval Training Station. With college teams nearly barren due to the war, the Pasadena Tournament of Roses agreed to a New Year's Day game in 1919 at the 5th Rose bowl between the Great Lakes Navy Bluejackets and the Mare Island Marines. Halas caught a 32-yard touchdown pass in the third quarter and also had a 77-yard interception return—a record that still stands for the longest interception return that wasn't a touchdown—in Rose Bowl history.

For his efforts, he was named the game's MVP. When he was out of the Navy, he played minor league baseball, seeing twelve games as an outfielder for the 1919 New York Yankees, going 2 for 22 (.091) at the plate. His most famous teammate is one of the best bits of baseball trivia of all-time, Wally Pipp. A strapping first baseman, Pipp was the Yankees' regular first baseman from 1915-1924. The Yankees got off to a slow start in 1925, and Pipp was part of the problem batting just .244 through 41 games. With the team 15-26, the manager opted to bench Pipp for one game for a rookie named Lou Gehrig. Gehrig got a hit and started the next game, and the next, and the next. He wound up with twenty home runs and 68 RBI while hitting .295 in two-thirds of a season. Pipp never got his job back, as Gehrig played in a then-record 2,130 straight games. Halas was no Gehrig, not even a Pipp, and he left baseball to play for the Hammond Pros, earning $75 per game back on the gridiron.

A year later, he was in Decatur working for starch manufacturer the A.E. Staley Company, where he did sales, played outfield on the company baseball team, and was player-coach of the company's Decatur Staleys. He took his college squad's colors—orange and navy blue—and made them into the Staleys. In 1920, just 25 years old, he represented the Staleys at the famous meeting that formed the American Professional Football Association in Canton. Two years later, the league became the NFL.

In his first year as coach, the Staleys went 10-1-2 but didn't draw crowds. The company founder turned the team over to Halas, and he moved them to Chicago, keeping the name in 1921 as they won the league championship. The title was a tainted one, as the Buffalo All-Americans had the best record (9-0-2) with Chicago finishing second (7-1-0). The two played in what Buffalo intended to be an exhibition game at the end of the year. Even after losing, Buffalo still had the best record, but Halas convinced two teams, Canton and the Chicago Cardinals, to finish with a better winning percentage and thus take the title from Buffalo.

In 1922, he renamed the Staleys as the Chicago Bears, a tribute to the town's popular baseball team, the Cubs.

Halas not only owned and coached the team, he also played wide receiver and defensive end. He was named to the 1920s all NFL team, but his most legendary moment came in 1923 when he stripped Jim Thorpe for a fumble and returned it 98 yards for a touchdown, a record that stood until 1972. In 1925, he recruited Red Grange to the Bears. He retired as player and coach in 1930 but stayed on as an owner and then went back to coaching in 1933, largely to eliminate the cost of having a head coach! He remained the coach for ten more years and introduced the infamous Wing-T offense to the sport in the late 1930s, which was so devastating it allowed the Bears to set two still-standing records when they blew out the Washington Redskins 73-0 in the 1940 NFL title game.

1927 New York Giants

Few teams before or since have dominated like the 1927 Giants did. The season came after a special meeting that eliminated the weaker teams, largely in the Midwest, and put more quality players on fewer dreams. The league dropped to twelve teams and the NFL became bigger on the East Coast, including two teams in New York City: Red Grange's Yankees and their rivals the New York Giants. The Giants had gone 8-4-1 the year before and finished sixth, but they had figured it out later, winning their last four games, all by shutout. The trend continued in their first three games of 1927 as they went 2-0-1 with wins of 8-0 over Providence, a 0-0 tie with Cleveland, and a 19-0 win over Pottsville. Their first loss was a narrow one, 6-0 to Cleveland, and then they reeled off five straight shutouts in 17 days.

They proved mortal by allowing a touchdown each to the Cardinals and Bears in 28-7 and 13-7 wins, and then blanked the Yankees twice 14-0 and 13-0 to win the league title. As their defensive prowess grew, so too did their popularity. The Giants drew 20,000 fans in their win over Pottsville in Week 7. A week later, 38,000 turned up to the Polo Grounds to watch them steamroll the Steam Roller.

For the season, the Giants finished 11-1-1 and outscored their opponents 197-20, allowing 1.5 points per season, the lowest total in NFL history. They won the league title by four games over Green Bay (7-2-1). Fullback Jack McBride scored 57 points for the team, rushing for six touchdowns and kicking fifteen extra points and two field goals. The team ranked first in yards allowed and yards gained as well. Earl Potteiger was the head coach.

Joe Guyon

At any other college, Joe Guyon would have been the best there ever was. When it came to Carlisle Indian Industrial School, he wasn't even the best guy on his own team. That's because Guyon played in the same era at the same school as Jim Thorpe, who many believe to be the greatest athlete this country has ever known. Guyon was an American Indian from the Chippewa tribe and was born in White Earth, Minnesota. Like Thorpe, he played under Pop Warner, but he was a left tackle, not a feature back. The 1912 team was amazing, scoring 454 points and going 12-1-1. The team played against Army, a squad featuring future US President Dwight D. Eisenhower and first-team all-American Leland DeVore, who would later become the Army's first motor transport officer. DeVore was so frustrated by Guyon that he was ejected from the game. When Thorpe left for the pros, Guyon took over as halfback and the team went 10-1-1. He was named a second-team all-American. He went on to play for Georgia Tech in 1917-1918 under a coach named John Heisman, whose name still echoes to this day. That 1917 team went 9-0, averaging 54.5 points per game and for years after was considered "the greatest the South ever produced." Guyon was absolutely unstoppable, with his first run of the season going 75 yards for a touchdown against Wake Forest. When Tech beat Vanderbilt 83-0, he rushed twelve times for 344 yards, a staggering 29 yards per carry, and against Tulane, all four members of Georgia Tech's backfield cleared 100 yards rushing. Guyon threw two touchdowns and ran for another one.

The 1918 team was less prolific, and Guyon split time at tackle and fullback. In 1919, he went pro and joined the Canton Bulldogs. From 1919-1924, he and Thorpe played side by side before Guyon went on to join the Kansas City Cowboys. He won a title with the 1927 New York Giants. When he wasn't smashing mouths on the field, he was coaching on the sideline. He coached the Union University Bulldogs in 1919 and returned to the school to coach all sports from 1923-1927. He also coached the St. Xavier high school team in Louisville, KY, from 1931-1933.

Like his fellow American Indian star Thorpe, Guyon was a model baseball player as well, hitting above .340 for three straight years in the American Association for the Louisville Colonels. He was a good baseball coach as well, leading Clemson from 1928-1931.

Jimmy Conzelman

There aren't many things Jimmy Conzelman couldn't do well. He was a great player, an amazing coach, a Navy man, a baseball executive, and an advertising guru. Born in St. Louis in 1898, he attended Loyola Academy and then Central High School. He started at Central High as a halfback and moved to McKinley High after a reorganization of the schools, competing in football, basketball, and track. He won a league title as a quarterback in 1915.

He moved on to Washington University in 1916, but entered the US Navy the following year. He was the quarterback of the 1918 Great Lakes Navy Bluejackets team that defeated not only Navy, which was undefeated up to that point, but also the Mare Island Marines by a 17-0 count in the 1919 Rose Bowl. Amazingly, Conzelman would play alongside two other future NFL hall of famers on that team—Paddy Driscoll and George Halas.

After the war, he went back to school and led Washington to a 5-2 record in 1919 as his team outscored opponents 127-30. He lost his ability to play the next year due to his grades, and when his stepfather died, he quit school altogether to help out his mother and younger brothers and sisters.

When the American Professional Football Association was born, he got back into the game, joining the Decatur Staleys, the precursor to the Chicago Bears. He was reunited there with former teammate George Halas. In his first game, he scored the only touchdown of the game on a 43-yard run. He started as halfback, punter, and placekicker, and also played quarterback as needed. The Staleys finished second with a 10-1-2 record.

The next year, he joined the Rock Island Independents as both captain and coach. At age 23 he was one of the youngest coaches in NFL history and led the team to a 4-1 record. He continued to do both playing and coaching the next year with the Milwaukee Badgers, leading them to a 7-2-3 record in 1923 and scoring four touchdowns and two extra points.

Within two years, he had traded hats and become the owner of the NFL franchise in Detroit, which he named the Panthers. It cost him just $50 to get the franchise—about $700 in today's money. He wore the hats of owner, player, and coach for the Panthers. The team went 8-2-2 and outscored its opponents 129-39. Attendance took a dive the next year, and Conzelman sold the team back to the league for $1,200. Conzelman still had the pigskin in his veins, however, and signed on as player, manager, and coach for the 1927 Providence Steam Roller. He scored four touchdowns and led the team to an 8-5-1 record, and the following year delivered Providence's first NFL title, going 8-1-2. He was the team MVP. In 1929, his team went 4-6-2, and Conzelman stepped away from playing.

He went on to coach independent and in college before returning to coach the Chicago Cardinals from 1940-1942. It was not a good fit, and the team went just 8-22. He left the NFL to become an administrator for the St. Louis Browns baseball team in 1943. He stayed two years working for owner Donald Brown and saw the team win the American league in 1944.

He went back to the Cardinals as a coach beginning in 1946. The success came about this time for Conzelman, as the Cardinals won the 1947 NFL Championship game over the Philadelphia Eagles, and went 11-1 in 1948, losing the title to the Eagles. Conzelman went 26-9 in his second three seasons with the team. He developed a passion for advertising later in life and unexpectedly resigned after the second NFL title game to take a role in D'Arcy Advertising Co. He was part of the NFL's second Hall of Fame class in 1964, and in 1968, a plaque honoring him was dedicated at Busch memorial Stadium in St. Louis.

He passed away in 1970 at age 72. In 2006, he was one of the eight charter members of the Arizona Cardinals Ring of Honor.

Paddy Driscoll

You don't get much more Midwest football than John Leo

"Paddy Driscoll." He was born in Evanston, Illinois, and died in Chicago. He went to school at Northwestern and played professionally for Hammond, Racine, and Chicago. He also coached the Bears as well as Marquette University. Driscoll weighed in at just 143 pounds in college, but that didn't stop him from being a fearless halfback. He scored nine points on a touchdown and a field goal as Northwestern defeated Chicago 10-0 in 1916, the first time the Wildcats had triumphed over their rivals in fifteen years. He also played on the basketball and baseball teams.

In fact, he was talented enough in baseball to play for the Chicago Cubs during the summer of 1917. It was a short-lived experiment, as Driscoll played just thirteen games, batting .107 with a double, three runs batted in, and a pair of stolen bases.

That fall, he joined the Hammond Clays and instantly became a star, leading the team to the Indiana Championship. The everyman Driscoll was a huge hit, starting in October 1917, when he scored all 20 of Hammond's points (three touchdowns, two extra points) in a 20-0 win over Wabash. One of his three touchdowns was a kickoff return for a touchdown to start the third quarter. Part of his legacy was his ability to drop kick the ball with incredible accuracy and distance. He was widely considered the best drop kicker of the early era. He scored all the team's points again in front of 5,000 people to defeat Pine Village 13-0. It was only the second loss Pine Village had suffered in twelve years.

A week later, Driscoll was knocked unconscious during the third quarter against Cornell. He would return to the field late in the game and drop kick a 55-yard field goal to seal up a 13-3 in. In the final game of the season, he scored three touchdowns and kicked an extra point in a 25-0 win over Fort Wayne.

Like many of his contemporaries, Driscoll wound up in the Navy in World War II and played alongside George Halas and Jimmy Conzelman. As a former pro player, Driscoll was denied the right to play for the Great Lakes Navy Bluejackets team. Eventually, he was allowed to join the team and made up for lost time in a 54-14 drubbing of Rutgers as he ran for six touchdowns and kicked five extra points. In the 1919 Rose Bowl, he drop kicked a field goal and threw a touchdown pass to Halas, who would become a lifelong friend. In the post-game write-up, the Los Angeles Times writer said, "Driscoll needs no praise. He is the greatest backfield start we have ever seen in Southern California and had at his command as fine a team of football players as any player could ask."

Weeks after the Rose Bowl win, he was traded by the Chicago Cubs to the Los Angeles Angels. He willingly went back to Southern California and played shortstop in the Pacific Coast League, hitting .264 with three doubles, four triples, and a home run.

That fall, he played for the Hammond All-Stars along with Halas. Playing at Wrigley Field, he returned a punt 50 yards for a touchdown, and kicked a field goal and three extra points.

The following season, he signed with the Racine Cardinals and was named a team captain. During this first year of the NFL, he helped the team to a 6-2-2 record. He wound up back at Wrigley field for a game against the Chicago Tigers. In front of 7,000 fans, he returned a punt for the winning touchdown in a 6-3 win. It wasn't his only game winner. That November, he kicked the winning extra point in a 7-6 win over Decatur. The Cardinals went 7-2-2 and finished fourth. Driscoll was named first-team all-quarterback.

In 1921, Driscoll was again captain and unofficial coach as well. In a 20-0 win over Minneapolis, he ran for a touchdown, threw for another, and kicked two extra points. That November, he made a 35-yard field goal with four minutes to play to forge a 3-3 tie with the Green Bay Packers. The Cardinals moved up to third in 1922, with an 8-3 record. The crowds got bigger and bigger as his legend grew. The Cardinals shutout the Bears twice in three weeks before crowds of 14,000 and 12,000. He had three field goals in the second win, a 9-0 slugfest.

Driscoll led the NFL in scoring in 1923, with 78 points put together on seven touchdowns, 10 field goals, and six extra points. He had 19 of those points in a 19-0 win over Akron. In the first five games of the season, he scored 69 points before getting hurt.

In 1924, Driscoll launched a 55-yard field goal in the first game of the year. The record stood for 29 years.

In 1925, the Cardinals finally broke through for the NFL title, going 12-2-1. Driscoll was again the leading scorer for the team, with 67 points on 11 field goals, four touchdowns, and 10 extra points. That November, the Cardinals took on the Chicago Bears before a capacity crowd of 36,000. It was the debut of Red Grange with the Bears, but Driscoll kept punting the ball away from him, drawing boos from the crowd. The Chicago Tribune praised Driscoll, saying he was "out there to win, not to let Grange stage a Roman holiday at their expense."

The next year, Driscoll was sold to the Bears and led them to a 12-1-3 record as he scored a career-high 86 points on six touchdowns, 12 field goals, and 14 extra points. The 12 field goals broke his own record. After coaching at the high school and college level, Driscoll was hired by longtime friend George Halas as an assistant coach with the Bears. He remained there until 1955, winning four NFL titles in the process. In 1956, he was hired by Halas as his own successor. He remained with the Bears in various roles until 1963, dying in 1968. Halas called Driscoll "the greatest athlete I ever knew."

Guy Chamberlain

A great player who became an even greater coach, the pride of Blue Springs, Nebraska, was among the most uniquely talented players in the early days of the NFL. He led the Nebraska Cornhuskers to consecutive Missouri Valley Conference championships and in 1936 was named the greatest player in Nebraska history.

He played pro football for nine years for seven teams and won championships in six of his nine seasons: as a player for the 1919 Canton Bulldogs and the 1921 Chicago Staleys, and as a player coach for the 1922-1924 Bulldogs, as well as the 1926 Frankford Yellow Jackets.

In six years as a head coach, he compiled a 58-16-7 record, the best record of any coach with a minimum of 50 wins. He's also the only coach to win the NFL title with three different teams. First a back, he moved to end in 1915 and caught 15 touchdown passes. He led the Huskers to a 20-19 thriller over Notre Dame and scored four touchdowns in his final college game, a 52-7 rout of Iowa. Remarkably, he went back to farming after graduation and was in the Army during World War II, stationed in Kentucky, Oklahoma, and San Diego.

He went back to football in 1919, playing for Jim Thorpe's Canton Bulldogs who went 9-0-1 that year. From there, he moved to George Halas' Decatur Staleys, who went 10-1-2 in 1920. The team moved to Chicago in 1921 and won the AFPA championship with a 9-1-1 record. Chamberlain's legend grew at the title game against Buffalo when he returned an interception 90 yards for the game-winning touchdown. He jumped to the Canton Bulldogs in 1922 and the team won the title with a 10-0-2 record, shutting out nine of twelve opponents and allowing only 15 points in 12 games. He led the team in scoring with seven touchdowns—two of them on interception returns.

Back to Canton in 1923, he remarkably won another title as the Bulldogs went 11-0-1 with eight shutouts and a combined total of 246 points for and 19 against.

Canton moved to Cleveland for the 1924 season, but Chamberlain was still the man, leading his team to a 7-1- record for a third straight title. He played and coached for the Frankford Yellow Jackets out of Philadelphia over the next two seasons, but injuries cost him several games. The 1926 Yellow Jackets went 14-1-2, shutting out 10 NFL opponents. He continued his playing career to the ripe old age of 33, playing for the Chicago Cardinals in 1927 while also serving as coach. A statue of Chamberlain sits at Southern Elementary School in Blue Springs, Nebraska.

FACTS AND FIGURES

1. The Muncie Flyers played in just one game in the inaugural season of the APFA, disbanding after being blown out 45-0 by the Rock Island Independents.

2. The Akron Pros allowed just 7 points in their 1920 inaugural season but still wound up with an 8-0-3 record. They tied Cleveland 7-7 and ended the season with consecutive 0-0 ties against Buffalo and Decatur.

3. The Green Bay Packers' first season in the APFA was 1921, as they went 3-2-1. The franchise has been in Green Bay ever since.

4. The Chicago Bears took their new form in the 1922 season, meaning they always trail Green Bay by one year in terms of longest-running franchise in the NFL.

5. By 1922, there were teams in all four of the modern-day NFC North cities—Chicago, Green Bay, Minneapolis, and Detroit.

6. Red Grange completed just 24 passes in his playing career, but 10 of those went for touchdowns.

7. Red Grange had two of the coolest nicknames in NFL history—the Galloping Ghost and the Wheaton Iceman.

8. With a career record of 58-16-7, Guy Chamberlain has the best winning percentage (.759) of any coach in NFL history with a minimum of 50 wins.

9. Guy Chamberlain remains the only coach in NFL history to win championships with three different teams.

10. The league was so top-heavy in 1925 that Dayton (0-7-1), Columbus (0-9-0), Duluth (0-3-0), Milwaukee (0-6-0), and Rochester (0-6-1) combined to go 0-31-2.

11. Paddy Driscoll scored more than 65 points three times in his career, including a career-high of 86 points in 1926.

12. Paddy Driscoll 55-yard field goal record, set in 1924, stood for 29 years until broken by Bert Rechichar in 1953. That record stood another 17 years until it was shattered by New Orleans' Tom Dempsey, who nailed a 63-yarder in 1970.

13. The Green Bay Packers became the first team in NFL history to win three straight titles in a row when they did so between 1929-1931.

14. The Packers went 34-5-2 in the span, a winning percentage of 85.4%.

15. The 1934 New York Giants became the first team with more than three losses to win the league title when they went 8-5 to win the East Division, then shocked the 13-0 Chicago Bears 30-13 in the title game.

TRIVIA QUESTIONS

1. How many teams participated in the first season of the APFA?

    A. 10
    B. 12
    C. 14
    D. 16

2. Who won the first APFA Championship?

    A. Chicago
    B. Akron
    C. Canton
    D. Columbus

3. How many points did the Hammond Pros score in their 1922 0-5-1 season?

    A. 0
    B. 3
    C. 6
    D. 14

4. What team was disqualified from winning the league title in 1925?

    A. Detroit
    B. Columbus

C. Akron

D. Pottsville

5. Which was the first team to win three straight NFL championships?

A. Canton

B. Chicago

C. Green Bay

D. New York

Answers

1. C
2. B
3. A
4. D
5. C

CHAPTER 2

RAPID EXPANSION
(1930S-1950S)

The Great Depression might have done in the NFL. It certainly reduced it to ten teams by the start of the 1931 season. But instead of becoming a footnote, the league banded together and only put franchises in markets that could support them. The number of teams dropped to eight by 1932, but a stroke of genius came thereafter with the splitting of the league into two divisions, each of which produced a champion to play in a title game at the end of the year. The introduction of the draft followed soon thereafter, as well as the first game on national TV. Racism reared its ugly head during this era, but by the 1950s, the game had outpaced its college equivalent in terms of popularity.

Playoff Fever

The New York Stock Exchange crashed on October 29, 1929, touching off the start of the Great Depression that lasted more than a decade before the United States turned its great factories back on to join the Allied cause in World War II. There were twelve teams in the NFL in 1929, but the number dropped to eleven in 1930 and to ten in 1931. The Boston Braves joined the fray in 1932, but Frankford and Providence collapsed, as did Cleveland, leaving the league with just eight teams—Boston, Brooklyn, two in Chicago, Green Bay, New York, Portsmouth, and Staten Island.

The 1932 season had ended in a dispute of who should play for the league title. The Chicago Bears were 6-1-6, the Green Bay Packers 10-3-1, and the Portsmouth Spartans were 6-1-4. The Packers had the highest winning percentage, but ties were thrown out of the standings, meaning Chicago and Portsmouth were both seen as 6-1 and Green Bay at 10-3. The Packers were left out of the playoff, which resulted in a 9-0 Bears triumph for the title.

The owners met before the season and agreed to split the league into two divisions. The winner of each division played in a title game, leaving no doubt who the best team in the league was. So it was that the league was split into the East division and the West division for the 1933 season. The East was comprised of the New York Giants, Brooklyn Dodgers, Washington Redskins, Philadelphia Eagles, and Pittsburgh Pirates, the West by the Chicago Bears, Portsmouth Spartans, Green Bay Packers, Cincinnati Reds, and Chicago Cardinals. There was no controversy this time as the Giants took the East by six games with an 11-3 mark and the Bears by 3-3 games with a 10-2-1 record. They clashed in the NFL Championship game the Sunday before Christmas, with the Bears eking out a 23-21 win in front of a crowd of 26,000 at Wrigley Field.

Bill Karr scored the second of his two second-half touchdowns on a 19-yard lateral to bring the Bears back to victory. In a clash of styles, the Bears' rushing attack (49 carries for 161 yards) overpowered the Giants' passing game (14-of-20 for 208 yards). It was a victory as well for 30-year-old Red Grange, who was in his second-to-last year in the NFL. The following year, the two teams would clash again, with the Bears entering the title game 13-0, having outscored opponents 286-86, while the Giants went 8-5, averaging just 11 points per game and relying on a resilient defense. The two teams had met a month earlier, with the Bears easily winning a 27-7 laugher as the Giants committed six turnovers. The rematch, played in front of more than 35,000 fans, saw the Giants put on one of the most shocking rallies in NFL history. Trailing 3-3 after three quarters, they exploded for 27 points in the fourth quarter as Ken Strong rushed for touchdowns of 42 and 11 yards and kicked 2 extra points. Ike Frankian caught a 28-yard pass from Ed Danowski, and Danowski scored on a nine-yard run. Each of Chicago's three quarterbacks threw an interception, and the Giants stuffed the Bears' vaunted rushing game, allowing them just 89 yards on 46 carries—an average of 1.93 yards per attempt. Meanwhile, the Giants gained 173 yards on 37 carries, led by Strong's 94 yards on just nine attempts. It was the final NFL game for Chicago's Red Grange.

Bronko Nagurski

It's hard to imagine someone having a better football name than Bronislau "Bronko" Nagurski. His parents were immigrants from Ukraine, and he was an all-American defensive tackle and fullback for three straight seasons at the University of Minnesota from 1927-1929. He was among the very unique class to be inducted into the Collegiate Hall of Fame and the Pro Football Hall of Fame in both legacies' first years of operation. Born in Canada, he was a timber worker in his teenage years, explaining his massive, muscular frame. His signature game was in college during the 1928 season, when he recovered a fumble as the Badgers were driving to seal the game, rushed six straight times for a touchdown, then intercepted a pass on defense to seal the win.

In his three seasons, the Gophers went 18-4-2 and won a Big Ten title game in 1927. At 6-feet, 2-inches and 235 pounds, Nagurski was bigger than most lineman in the NFL, wearing a size 19 ring, the largest ever produced in the NFL, and a size 8 helmet. In 1932, he threw the game-winning touchdown pass to Red Grange as the Bears beat the Portsmouth Spartans to win the NFL title. The next year, he won a second crown with Chicago. While stats were not kept outside of touchdowns during his first two seasons, Nagurski was a hit from the get-go, starting all thirteen games as a rookie in 1930 and scoring five touchdowns. He was a bulldozer from the get-go, never averaging more than 4.8 yards per carry but piling up the touchdowns, including seven during the Bears' 1934 undefeated regular season.

During the off-season from football, Nagurski became a successful professional wrestler and also a movie star. He held five different wrestling titles during his career and was enshrined in the Wrestling Hall of Fame in 2011. He retired from the Bears in 1937 at age 29, only to return to the team in what can only be described as a tale straight out of a comic book or a bit of mythology. In 1943, six years after his final game, he returned to the Bears, who like every NFL team, had a roster void of its former players because of the US' involvement in World War II. He played in eight games but still had the magic, averaging 5.3 yards per carry. The Bears went 8-1-1 to win their division and defeated the Washington Redskins 41-21 in the NFL title game, with Nagurski carrying the ball eleven times for 34 yards and scoring a touchdown.

World War II and the NFL

Bravery in football pales to bravery in combat. When the US declared war on Japan and then Germany late in the 1940s, players and even some coaches were drafted or volunteered by the dozens. When the Brooklyn Dodgers opened training camp in the summer of 1942, only seven of their players were left. The Cleveland Rams suspended play for the 1943 season, while the Pittsburgh Steelers and Philadelphia Eagles combined forces to become the Steagles, splitting home games between the two cities in 1943. The Steelers and Chicago Cardinals merged in 1944, and the Boston Yanks merged with Brooklyn for the 1945 season.

Twenty-one men associated with the NFL were killed in combat during World War II—nineteen of them active or former players—along with an ex-head coach and a team executive. Three members of the military—Maurice Britt, Joe Foss, and Jack Lummus—were all awarded the Congressional Medal of Honor, the highest military honor in the United States. Britt played for the Detroit Lions in 1941, then headed for war as a second lieutenant in Arkansas after the season. He was a platoon leader during the invasion of Sicily in 1943. During Operation Shingle, he did exercises in plain sight of enemy lines to expose the location of a hidden Nazi machine gun nest. He earned the Distinguished Service Cross for this act of heroism and was the first recipient of the top four combat decorations for valor awarded an infantryman in World War II. He later became lieutenant governor of his home state of Arkansas.

Foss was a Marine pilot who claimed twenty-six enemy fighters during the Second World War He was later elected Governor of South Dakota and served as commissioner of the AFL from

1960-1966.

Jack Lummus played college at Baylor University and was an outstanding baseball and football player. He played for the New York Giants on the gridiron in 1941. After that year's title game, he enlisted in the Marine Corps reserves. Three years later, he was one of the first wave of troops to land at Iwo Jima. Two weeks into the assault, after clearing out three enemy strongholds, Lummus stepped on a landmine and lost both legs in the explosion. Despite surgery and a blood transfusion of eighteen pints, he died on the operating table. His commanding officer wrote to his mother, *"Jack suffered very little, for he didn't live long. I saw Jack soon after he was hit. With calmness, serenity, and complacency, Jack said, 'The New York Giants lost a good man.' We all lost a good man."*

Among active players, the face of the war was Giants' tackle Al Blozis, who volunteered although he could have stayed home because his size—6 feet 6 inches, 250 pounds—was outside the scope of the draft. He had been a world-class shot-putter at Georgetown and set an US Army record for the longest grenade throw. Just six weeks after playing in the NFL title game, he was killed by German machine gunfire while searching for a missing patrol in the mountains of France.

And one final note: While he would not be known to the NFL at large for many years, there was also a 19-year-old University of Texas freshman who enlisted in the Army Air Corps to fight the good fight. He was stationed in London and flew thirty missions, even surviving a crash landing in Belgium. His name? Tom Landry.

The Rams Go West

The Cleveland Browns got their start in the AFL in 1936 before moving to the NFL from 1937-1945. They were generally terrible those first few years, going 1-0 in 1937, with their only non-losing record from 1937-1944 coming in 1939 when they went 5-5-1. With World War II winding down, the Rams were suddenly looking up in 1945. Pat Waterfield arrived to play quarterback after four years at UCLA and was named the NFL MVP in his first season after being drafted in the fifth round. Waterfield led the league in offense with 1,627 yards, as well as in touchdown passes (14) and average yards per completion (9.4). On Thanksgiving Day, he torched the Detroit Lions for 339 yards. That game also saw end Jim Benton become the first player in NFL history to record 300 yards receiving a game, with 303 on 10 receptions. His record stood until 1985.

After years as a doormat, the Rams swept the Bears (17-0 and 41-21), beat the Giants on the road (20-7), and swept the Packers (27-14 and 20-7). Their only loss was 28-14 at Philadelphia. The win over the Lions won them the division title, and they followed with one of the most exciting title games in the short history of the league, edging Washington 15-14 as

Waterfield threw two touchdowns in front of a crowd of 32,000. Waterfield was married to Hollywood actress Jane Russell. A month after the title, Rams' owner Dan Reeves shocked fans and his fellow owners by announcing the team would move to Los Angeles, the first NFL team west of the Mississippi River. Reeves had wanted to move the team since buying in in 1941, and was fearful of the incoming Cleveland Browns of the All-America Football Conference, as former Ohio State coach Paul Brown coached them. The move pained Cleveland but had a huge impact, as part of the condition of the team renting the Los Angeles Memorial Coliseum was the promise to use African-American players. It was hard to resist the lure of doing business in LA. The population had grown from 319,198 in 1910 to 1.5 million in 1940. By 1950, another 380,000 people had been added to the mix, and by 1960 the population was at 2.479 million.

The team went 6-4-1 in its first year but only hovered around .500 until 1949 when they went 8-2-2, winning the West and falling to the Philadelphia Eagles in the title game, 14-0. In 1950, two extra playoff games were held as the Browns and Giants tied for the East title and Rams and the Bears for the West. The Rams defeated Chicago 24-14, but the city of Cleveland got a taste of revenge at their departed Rams. The Browns won a 30-28 thriller on Christmas Eve, rallying from a 28-20 deficit with 10 unanswered points in the fourth quarter. The Browns' Otto Graham was a one-man wrecking crew, completing 22-of-33 passes for 298 yards and four touchdowns, and rushing for another 99 yards on 12 carries. The 1951 season saw a new quarterback for Los Angeles, as Norm Van Brocklin took over, and the Rams in an intense division title that saw them take the national title with an 8-4 record, just ahead of 7-4-1 Detroit, 7-4-1 San Francisco, and 7-5 Chicago. Waterfield and Van Brocklin combined to throw for 3,291 yards and 26 touchdowns. The Rams faced the Browns again for the title, and won the title on a 73-yard touchdown pass from Van Brocklin to Tom Fears.

The Ugly Face of Racism

Black players had a face in the early days of the APFA and the NFL, with nine suiting up. The success of the Carlisle Indian School football team, including the legendary Jim Thorpe, opened the gateways of the league to other Native Americans. The Dayton Triangles employed Asian-Americans Walter Achiu and Arthur Matsu, and Hispanic players Ignacio Molinet and Jess Rodriguez were in the league as early as 1927. Suddenly, after the 1927 season, every black player was kicked out of the league without explanation, and not one played in the NFL from 1928-1932. One of those two was Fritz Pollard, who, along with Bobby Marshall, were the first two African American players in the NFL. Pollard was the first black player at Brown University, where he studied Chemistry, and he was a starting halfback as Brown won the 1916 Rose Bowl. Two black men, Joe Lillard and Ray Kemp, were in the league in 1933, but Lillard was kicked off the Cardinals for fighting, and Kemp left on his own to pursue coaching. He played for the Akron Pros, who won the AFPA Championship in 1921, and was the coach of the Hammond Pros in 1923-1924.

A large part of the movement to keep black players out of the league was the work of Washington Redskins owner George Preston Marshall. Black players were excluded from the NFL until 1946, when the Los Angeles Rams were forced to reintegrate as part of the deal to rent the Los Angeles Coliseum, their new home. The Rams signed Kenny Washington and Woody Strode, and by 1949, other teams began using draft picks on African-Americans. Not Marshall, however, who said he would start hiring "coloreds when the Harlem Globetrotters started hiring whites." Finally, in 1962, Marshall met his match in the form of US Attorney General Robert F. Kennedy. The Redskins' 30-year lease on D.C. Stadium was up. The stadium was owned by the Washington D.C. government. Kennedy said unless Marshall hired a black player, the government who revoke his lease. Marshall finally acquiesced and drafted Syracuse All-American running back Ernie Davis as his #1 pick. Davis knew the situation and demanded a trade, with the Redskins getting African-American All-Pro Bobby Mitchell, who grew into a Hall of Fame wide receiver.

The All-America Football Conference

The NFL took off after World War II, and suddenly professional football was on the tongue of every businessman in the country. While the NFL had a limited number of franchises, the number of players coming out of college was enormous, and that was enough for Chicago Tribune sports editor Arch Ward, who founded the league in June of 1944, bringing in a number of wealthy investors who had previously tried and failed to get franchises of their own. Ward had previously advised the NFL to expand but was rebuffed. Instead, he formed the All-America Football Conference (AAFC) with teams in Buffalo, Chicago, Cleveland, Los Angeles, New York, and San Francisco. Miami and Brooklyn came later. The league planned to open in 1945, but waited another year after the end of World War II. The league opened just a year after the city of Cleveland had lost the Rams to Los Angeles after winning a title.

In their place came the Browns, with Coach Paul Brown, who had won six high school championships in Ohio at Massillon High School and the 1942 national championship at Ohio State. The NFL was threatened by the new league, especially Redskins' owner George Marshall, who saw his coach and many players depart for the new Baltimore entry in 1946.The AAFC was popular right away. Arch had power in the press to give tons of publicity, the league signed 40 of the 66 College All-Stars, and air travel had come into viable play, allowing the league to place teams in Florida and California. The league's first game was played September 6, 1946, as 60,000 people showed up to watch the Browns drub the Miami Seahawks 44-0. It was the largest pro football crowd to date. The league was largely successful, and Cleveland beat the New York Yankees 14-9 for the first title. NFL popularity rose as well, and the two leagues started competing heavily for players, sending salaries through the roof. For all the big crowds, only two teams made a profit in pro football in 1946—the Browns and the Bears.

An even bigger year for the AAFC was 1947. The 49ers secured the rights to Army's Mr. Inside, Felix Blanchard, and Mr. Outside, Glenn Davis. A game between the New York Yankees and Los Angeles Dons drew 82,000 people in Los Angeles, and the Browns defeated the Yankees for the title. It was broken the next year when the 9-0 Browns defeated the 10-0 49ers in front of 83,000 people in Cleveland. The Browns won a third straight title, and the problem became obvious—the league was quite top heavy. One team folded in 1947, dropping the AAFC to seven. Cleveland won a fourth straight title and improved to 52-4-3 all-time. In late 1949, the two leagues merged. The Browns, 49ers, and Colts joined the NFL and the Dons merged with the Rams. A few months later, the World Series of Pro Football was held between the NFL champion Eagles and the AAFC champion Browns. To the shock of the 71,000 fans on hand in Philadelphia that day, the Browns scored a rollicking 36-10 win. The next year, the Browns beat the Rams in the NFL title game for their fifth consecutive championship.

Sammy Baugh

The pride of Temple, Texas, Sammy Baugh was one of the first great quarterbacks in NFL history. He won two titles, was named to the first-team, All-Pro six times, and led the league in passing yardage four times and in passing touchdowns twice. He was also a devastating punter, and remarkably led the league in defensive interceptions, with eleven in 1943. His average of 51.4 yards per punt in 1940 is still the NFL record today.

Ironically, he really wanted to play pro baseball and signed a scholarship with Washington State University, only to hurt his knee sliding into second base a month before he was bound for school, and the scholarship was revoked.

He chose TCU instead and was a two-time All-American and MVP of the very first Cotton Bowl. In the spring of his senior year, George Marshall offered Baugh $4,000 to play for the Redskins. He was still aspiring to play pro baseball and did not take the deal until after the college All-Star Game, where the collegians beat the Green Bay Packers 6-0. He was the #6 pick in the 1937 NFL draft and ended up signing of $8,000. In his rookie year, he led the Redskins to the NFL title, setting a record for completions in a season with 91. Against the Bears, he was 17 of 33 for 335 yards and touchdown passes of 55, 78, and 33 in the 28-21 win.

Baugh was not drafted during World War II and took the

Redskins to a second title in 1942, defeating the Bears 14-6. He threw a touchdown pass and also launched an 85-yard punt. In 1943, Baugh had arguably the greatest individual season in NFL history, leading the league in passing, punting, and interceptions. In 1947, on Sammy Baugh Day in Washington D.C., he threw for 355 yards and six touchdowns. At the time of his retirement in 1952, he owned thirteen NFL records. He went on to coach the AFL's New York Titans and Houston Oilers. He passed away in 2008, the last surviving member of the 1963 inaugural Hall of Fame class.

Sid Luckman

Sid Luckman was the greatest Wing-T quarterback of all time, an NFL MVP, and the author of four Chicago Bears NFL titles between 1939 and 1950. He was originally drafted by the Steelers but traded to the Bears. Luckman actually had to be convinced by Halas to even play football, thinking he would work for his father-in-law's trucking company. When Halas came to Luckman's apartment with a contract for $5,000, things changed quickly. In his second season, Luckman led the title game against the Washington Redskins. The Skins had won their first matchup 7-3, but in the weeks since, Luckman, Halas, and offensive coordinator Clark Shaughnessy had added a "man-in-motion" wrinkle to the T-formation, one that the Redskins couldn't figure out. The Bears rushed the ball 53 times for 381 yards while holding the Redskins to five yards on 15 attempts. The Redskins turned the ball over nine times in a 73-0 loss, the most lopsided score in NFL history.

After the end of the 1943 season, Luckman volunteered as an ensign for the US Merchant Marines. He received permission to play for the Bears while stationed stateside but could not practice with them. Despite that, he led the league in passing in both 1945 and 1946 despite starting just seven of the 21 games he played in. He led the league in touchdown passes both years as well. In 1943, he led the league in yardage (2,194) and touchdown passes (28). His career average of 8.4 yards per attempt is second all-time to Otto Graham. He led the team to further titles in 1941, 1943, and 1946, and still holds two Chicago Bear passing records despite the fact that his career ended in 1950.

Chuck Bednarik

Chuck Bednarik was one of the nastiest SOBs to ever play professional football. The #1 pick of the 1949 NFL draft, he played all thirteen seasons with the Philadelphia Eagles, was an eight-time Pro Bowler, ten-time first-team All Pro and two-time NFL champion. Before he ever got to the NFL, however, he entered the Air Force and flew 30 combat missions over Nazi Germany, being awarded the Air Medal, four Oak Leaf clusters, the European-African Middle Eastern Campaign Medal, and four Battle Stars. From there, he went to Penn as a three-time

All-American at center, linebacker, and punter. In 1969, he was voted the greatest center of all time. He was the last full-time player in NFL history. In a game played in bitter rainy conditions in 1949, his Eagles stifled the Los Angeles Rams 14-0 for the NFL title, capping a 12-1 season for Philadelphia.

Bednarik was 35 years old before the Eagles won their second title, but his 1960 season is arguably his most famous. At 6 feet, 3 inches, and 233 pounds he was a true giant of the game. In 1960, during an Eagles-Giants game, he leveled Giants' running back/receiver Frank Gifford, an eight-time Pro Bowler and the league's MVP in 1956. It took Gifford eighteen months to recover from the hit and he retired from the NFL the following year. He returned in 1962 and played three more years but never again as a running back. A few months later, in the NFL title game, the Eagles led Green Bay 17-13. Packer running back Jim Taylor got loose, but Bednarik hauled him down in the open field at the 8-yard line, and lay on top of him while the final few seconds ticked off the clock to deliver the title.

Night Train Lane

Richard "Night Train" Lane was the epitome of everything that racist Redskins' owner George Marshall feared about African-American players coming into the NFL. Lane wasn't just good, he was unbelievable. After four years in the Army, he was working at an aircraft plant in Los Angeles, lifting heavy sheets of metal. He rode the bus every day to work and rode past the offices of the Los Angeles Rams. He had a scrapbook of clips from high school and junior college days and wanted to try out as a wide receiver but was moved to defensive back. In his first scrimmage, head coach Joe Stydahar said, "Lane came out here to make the ball club. Well, last night he got himself a job."

He didn't initially like his nickname of Night Train, thinking it a bit racist, but it really came from a record by Jimmy Forrest that he liked dancing to. He took more of a shine to it when a newspaper recorded quite possibly the greatest sports headline every after Lane destroyed Redskins star Choo Choo Justice, and the paper ran with "Night Train Derails Choo Choo." In his rookie year of 1952, Lane played twelve games and had fourteen interceptions, a still-standing NFL record. He had two returns for touchdowns, including an 80-yarder, and led the league with 298 yards of interception returns. In January 1954, he was traded to the Chicago Cardinals and again led the league in picks, this time with ten. After that, teams simply stopped throwing to his side of the field, making him that much more dangerous. He was traded again to the Lions in 1960, and in their first victory of the season, he intercepted a Johnny Unitas pass and returned it 80 yards for a touchdown.

FACTS AND FIGURES

1. In their dramatic victory in the 1934 NFL title games, the New York Giants scored more points in the fourth quarter (27) than they had in 11 of their 12 prior games.

2. Sammy Baugh's 335 yards passing in the NFL title game in 1937 stood as a postseason rookie record until 2012.

3. Baugh was drafted by the MLB's St. Louis Cardinals, but quit when he didn't receive enough playing time in Double A.

4. In a 1943 win over Detroit, Sammy Baugh threw four touchdown passes on offense and had four interceptions on defense.

5. In 1945 Sammy Baugh completed 70.33% of his passes (128 of 182), a record that stood until it was broken by Ken Anderson (70.55) in 1982.

6. Chuck Bednarik missed only three games in his 14 seasons.

7. The Chuck Bednarik Award is given annually to the best defensive player in college football.

8. Night Train Lane and Don Doll, the player he was traded for, are the only two players in NFL history with more than one season of 10+ interceptions.

9. Lane blocked an extra point and had a 42-yard interception return for a touchdown in the 1962 Pro Bowl. The next day he had his appendix removed.

10. Lane's fearsome tackle by the face mask Jon Arnett led to the league changing the rules the following year and outlawing grasping the face mask.

11. In 1944, the Brooklyn Dodgers changed their team name to the Tigers.

12. The Boston Yanks went bankrupt in 1949.

13. The first incarnation of the Baltimore Colts folded after its first year in the NFC (1950).

14. The Dallas Texans were born out of the ashes of the New York Yanks, only to fold after one season.

15. The Baltimore Colts joined the league again in 1953.

TRIVIA QUESTIONS

1. Who won the initial NFL title game in 1933?

    A. Chicago Bears
    B. New York Giants
    C. Philadelphia Eagles
    D. Pittsburgh Pirates

2. Who broke Sammy Baugh's record of 335 yards passing by a rookie in a playoff game?

    A. Dan Marino
    B. Peyton Manning
    C. Russell Wilson
    D. Matt Ryan

3. What team did George Halas convince to draft and trade him Sid Luckman?

    A. Rams
    B. Steelers
    C. Browns
    D. Giants

4. How many times in his 14-year career did Night Train Lane not have an interception over the course of the season?

    A. Zero

B. One

C. Two

D. Three

5. How many teams were in the NFL at the end of 1959?

   A. 10

   B. 14

   C. 12

   D. 16

Answers

1. A
2. C
3. B
4. B
5. C

CHAPTER 3

THE RIVAL (AFL, 1960-1969)

The NFL had successfully absorbed one league in the 1940s, but a more powerful arrived in the 1960s, one backed by billionaires who laid out smart strategies, played to the media, and gave fans what they wanted—high-scoring, well-played games featuring the top talent from the college game.

Formation

Max Winter was a successful restaurant owner and GM of the Minneapolis Lakers. He tried and failed in the 1950s to get an expansion NFL team to Minneapolis. Bob Howsam had tried to get Major League baseball to come to Denver in the 1950s and failed, so he turned to football when he realized how much debt he was in without a sports team to pay it off. Bud Adams Jr. was chairman and CEO of Adams resources & Energy, a wholesale supplier of oil and natural gas, and owned several Lincoln-Mercury dealerships. After World War II, he found himself stuck in Houston, Texas, after his plane got grounded by fog. He explored the city, found it to his liking, and started a wildcatting firm. He and fellow oil man Lamar Hunt tried to buy the Chicago

Cardinals and move them to Dallas, but the Cardinal ownership refused them.

Hunt's father was a millionaire himself and masterminded the creation of a rival football league in the summer of 1959. Hunt was convinced that regional rivalries would be the way to get the league off the ground and functioning quickly at a high level. On August 14, 1959, in Chicago, the charter memberships were given to Dallas, New York, Houston, Denver, Los Angeles, and Minneapolis-St. Paul. The league was named the American Football League eight days later in Dallas. The NFL tried its best to undermine the new league by changing its expansion policy, and the Minnesota Vikings jumped ship, joining the NFL in 1961. The AFL scored a major coup when it hired Joe Foss, an NFL vet and war hero—not to mention the former governor of South Dakota—to be its first commissioner. The Oakland Raiders replaced Minneapolis, and another team, the Boston Patriots, joined just in time for the draft. It lasted 33 rounds and a second 20-round draft came later.

Houston Oilers, Original Champions

With its initial territorial draft pick in 1960, the Houston Oilers went big, drafting LSU all-American and Heisman Trophy winner Billy Cannon Jr. He agreed to a $100,000 contract with the Oilers despite already signing a $50,000 deal with the NFL's Los Angeles Rams. The Oilers filed a lawsuit saying Cannon had been manipulated by LA's general manager, Pete Rozelle, and the court sided with Houston. To pair with their young running back, the Oilers signed a quarterback most teams thought as over the hill. George Blanda was 33 in 1960, having been out of football since 1958, and having not started a game since 1954. He had played as the Bears' backup throughout the 50s and had one great year in 1953, leading the league in completions and attempts and throwing for 2,164 yards.

The Oilers felt they were getting a 2-for-1 in Blanda, who was an experienced leader with years left on his arm from a lack of play in Chicago, and a world-class kicker with outstanding leg strength. Blanda started eleven of fourteen games for the Oilers in 1960 and went 8-3, throwing for 2,413 yards and 24 touchdowns. He also kicked 15 field goals and hit 46 of 47 extra points. Cannon and fullback Dave Smith combined to rush for 1,287 yards, and the Oilers were the best offense in the game, scoring 37 and 38 points in their first two games and leading the league at 27.1 points per game. On New Year's Day 1961, the Oilers hosted the Chargers in the first AFL title game. Despite 165 yards and a touchdown on the ground from Charger running back Paul Lowe, the Oilers won 24-16. Clinging to a one-point lead in the fourth quarter, Blanda hit Cannon on an 88-yard touchdown pass. Blanda threw for 301 yards and three touchdowns while Cannon had 178 all-purpose yards.

The Oilers and Chargers met again the following year for the title, although the Chargers had since moved to San Diego. When Houston got off to a 1-3-1 start, Adams pulled the plug on head coach Lou Rymkus and brought in Wally Lemm. The team responded with nine straight wins and cracked 500 totals points in fourteen games, putting up 55 twice and averaging 44.4 points per game in their last four games of the regular season. Blanda was a beast, throwing for 3,330 yards and 36 touchdowns, and Cannon had 1,534 total yards and 15 touchdowns. Blanda hit 64 of 65 extra points and kicked 16 field goals. The Chargers proved a tough out again in the title game, limiting Houston's offense like none other. The two teams combined for a horrific 13 turnovers as Blanda threw six interceptions. He also made a 46-yard field goal in the first half and hit Cannon for a 35-yard touchdown in the third quarter to provide the winning margin in a 10-3 slugfest.

Houston very nearly made it three straight titles when they took on the Dallas Texans in the 1962 AFL title game, still the longest American professional football game on record. Houston went 11-3 in the regular season with another dominant offense, scoring 56 in a rout of the New York Titans. Fullback Charley Tolar became the offense's prime weapon, rushing for 1,012 yards and 7 touchdowns. The title game pitted the two Texas teams against each other in front of 37,981 fans at Jeppesen Stadium in Houston. Astronaut Gus Grissom off Gemini 3 fame put the ball on the tee for the opening kickoff. Grissom would die tragically just five years later during a test launch of Apollo 1. Down 17-0 at halftime, the

Oilers rallied back to tie the game at 17, but a 42-yard Blanda field goal attempt in the final seconds was blocked. The first overtime featured a historic gaffe that could have cost the Texans dearly when Abner Haynes botched the coin toss in overtime. Wanting to take advantage of the wind, he meant to say he wanted the Texans to defend the end zone with the wind at their backs. Instead he said "We'll kick to the clock," which meant Dallas would kick off and Houston selected the end. The Oilers had the wind but couldn't do anything with it, and Dallas won on a short field goal three minutes into the second overtime. The two teams had played just shy of 78 minutes of football. The Oilers would join the NFL in 1970 and move to Tennessee in 1997. Despite several remarkable teams, they have never won another title since that 1961 season.

TV deal and the signing of Joe Namath

If NFL owners thought the AFL was just the latest upstart, they got a rude awakening in June of 1960 when the league signed a 5-year TV contract with ABC for $125,000. Attendance was poor at the games—about 16,500 per team per home game—and the Raiders nearly went bankrupt save for a $40,000 loan from Buffalo owner Ralph Wilson. The Chargers couldn't compete with the Rams in Los Angeles, so they bolted (pun intended) south for San Diego. The New York Titans had so few people at games that the owner moved the seats closer to the field so the stadium looked fuller. The Texans moved to Kansas City and became the Chiefs in 1963, and the Titans went bankrupt, with the league taking over until new management could be found, changing the name to the Jets. With decent TV ratings its first few years on a rival network, NBC decided to get into the game and the AFL signed a $36 million deal with the peacock in January of 1964. Pittsburgh Steelers owner Art Rooney was among those who recognized quickly that the AFL had rapidly caught up in a few years time to a league that had more than four decades in the book. They don't have to call us Mister anymore,' he famously said.

In November 1964, more than 61,000 fans showed up to watch the Jets and Bills play, an AFL record. The Jets stayed in the limelight that same year when they drafted University of Alabama quarterback Joe Namath. The Cardinals had done likewise in the NFL draft, but New York ponied up $427,000 and a new car to Namath and he jumped at it, becoming the richest collegiate draft pick ever. That same year, the AFL expanded twice to cities rebuffed by the NFL, birthing the Atlanta Falcons and Miami Dolphins. Namath wasn't great at the start, but got better quickly, leading the league in his second and third seasons with 3,379 and then 4,007 yards passing. One of his offensive linemen dubbed him Broadway Joe, and he appeared on the cover of Sports Illustrated the summer before his first season. He was the first quarterback to throw for more than 4,000 yards in a season, and that number stood as rookie record until Dan Fouts broke it in 16 games in 1979.

The merger

Foss had tried to get the NFL to talk about a merger or a championship game in 1963 and was rebuffed. Foss resigned as commissioner in April 1966, and was replaced by Raiders' head coach and general manager, Al Davis. Davis began luring NFL quarterbacks to the AFL for big contracts and had seven signed within the first two months of his time as the commissioner. A series of secret meetings followed as the NFL owners wanted to talk a merger. On June 8, 1966, it came to life, with the two teams coming together for the 1970 season as a 28-team league with Pete Rozelle as commissioner. Davis would remain the Raiders owner.

In the four-year span before the merger, a championship game would be played between the two leagues. The first such game came on January 15, 1967, dubbed the World Championship Game, played in Los Angeles between the NFL champion Green Bay Packers and the AFL champ Kansas City Chiefs. The Packers had won the NFL West with a 12-2 record, more than doubling up their opponents in scoring. The NFL title game was a 34-27 thriller that saw Bart Starr throw for 304 yards and four touchdowns to outduel Don Meredith. The Chiefs had won the AFL West by three games with an 11-2-1 record, racking up 448 points in the process. Future Hall of Famer quarterback Len Dawson threw for 26 touchdowns against just 10 interceptions, and the Chiefs steamrolled Buffalo 31-7 in the AFL title game as

Mike Garrett ran for two touchdowns. The first title game proved to be exactly as the NFL had expected and the AFL had feared. Up 14-10 at halftime, the Packers outscored the Chiefs 21-0 the rest of the way to cruise to a 35-10 victory. The Packer defense held the Chiefs to just 72 yards rushing and sacked Dawson six times. Packer legend Vince Lombardi said after the game, "I do not think they are as good as the top teams in the National Football League," which is about as close to trash talk as Lombardi got in his entire life. The next year was more of the same as the Packers blasted the Oakland Raiders 33-14.

The Heidi Bowl

The AFL was fighting its inferiority complex tooth and nail after the two Super Bowl blowouts. In 1968, there were several strong teams in the AFL, including the New York Jets and Oakland Raiders. Played on national television and hosted by the Raiders, the game was scheduled to run from 4-7 p.m. ET, after which the NBC network would run the popular children's movie Heidi to draw in a big nighttime audience. Unlike today, very few NFL games lasted longer than 2-3 hours. There were fewer timeouts and fewer TV timeouts. This Raiders-Jets game was an exception, marred by several injuries and a flurry of fourth-quarter scoring. The Jets and Raiders were both 7-2 entering the game and were bitter rivals. The Jets kicked a late field goal to go up 32-29 with a few minutes left, but 7 p.m. had come. Having sold two hours of advertising to Timex, NBC's head of programming made the call and cut the feed to the game. After a lengthy commercial break, football fans were horrified when instead of the next kickoff they saw a little girl frolicking in the hills of Europe. NBC phone lines lit up and virtually destroyed the whole network's phone banks as fuse after fuse exploded from thousands of complaints. Even worse, the Raiders went ahead 36-32 on a 43-yard Daryle Lamonica touchdown pass moments later. The Jets had a chance to tie the game but fumbled the kickoff, and the Raiders returned it for a score. In the span of mere minutes, a 32-29 Jets' lead had become a 43-32 Raiders' win. NBC took another gamble, running a sports bulletin across the bottom of the screen of the movie, terribly picking the scene where Heidi's paralyzed cousin Clara takes her first steps. Now movie fans were calling NBC in a rage. NBC made a policy the very next week that any game would show to its conclusion in its home markets.

The Guarantee

The AFL had received its merger, but the lack of respect was tangible after the first two Super Bowls saw the Packers rout the Chiefs and Raiders. The Packers slipped back to the pack in 1968, but the NFL saw a new power rise in the Baltimore Colts, who went 13-1 during the regular season. Led by young coach Don Shula, 38, the Colts outscored their opponents 402-144 and entered the postseason on an eight-game win streak. Quarterback Johnny Unitas had given way to Earl Morrall, who threw for 2,909 yards and 26 touchdowns on the year. The real strength was the defense, which had three all-pros and which racked up 29 interceptions and 23 fumble recoveries during the regular season, more than two interceptions a game.

They beat Minnesota 24-14 in the division round then crushed Cleveland 34-0 as Tommy Matte rushed for three straight touchdowns. Played outside with a 13-degree wind chill, Cleveland was held to 12 first downs. The New York Jets went 11-3 in 1968, scoring 29.9 points per game. They topped 30 points seven times and went for 47 and 48 in routs of the Boston Patriots. Namath threw for 3,147 yards and 15 touchdowns and was named league MVP. In the AFL title game, the Jets edged their fiercest rival, the Oakland Raiders, 27-23 on a late touchdown throw by Namath.

What followed was the first title game to bear the name Super Bowl, and it was held in Miami. Swaggering Namath went on the offensive with his mouth in the lead-up, saying there were five quarterbacks in the AFL better than Baltimore's Morrall. Three days before the game, Namath spoke to the Miami Touchdown Club and told the audience, "We're gonna win the game. I guarantee it." Namath's assessment of Morrall appeared accurate, as the quarterback threw three interceptions and was yanked in the second half for Unitas. Matt Snell scored a first-quarter touchdown, and Jim Turner scored 10 points on three field goals and an extra point to make it 16-0. Snell should have been MVP with 161 total yards and the touchdown, but Namath won it with 206 yards passing and no turnovers. Baltimore committed five turnovers as Namath swaggered off into sunset.

Weeb Ewbank

When you've got a name like Weeb Ewbank, you better be damn good at something if you don't want to get made fun of. Weeb was a damn good football coach. Ewbank cut his teeth under one of the greatest coaches the game has ever seen, Paul Brown, while both were in the Navy during World War II. He coached in college for three years then joined Brown with the Cleveland Browns and won an AAFC championship and the NFL championship in 1949. He left Brown's squad to become head coach of the Colts in 1954. He suffered new coach struggles just as every other man has, going 3-8, 5-6-1, and 5-7 in his first three seasons before getting the team to 7-5 in 1957. The next season, the Colts put it all together, racing out to a 6-0 start in which they scored more than 40 points three times including a staggering 56-0 rout of the Green Bay Packers in early November. Johnny Unitas, aged 25, started nine games and went 8-1, throwing for 2,007 yards and 19 touchdowns. He had an amazing array of targets, including right halfback Lenny Moore, who caught 50 passes for 938 yards and 7 touchdowns, and left end Raymond Berry, who caught 56 for 794 yards and 9 TDs. The Colts won a thrilling 23-17 overtime win over the Giants for the NFL title.

The Colts struggled out of the gate in 1959, starting 4-3 and losing back-to-back nail biters to the Redskins and Browns. Ewbank's group turned it around from there, rattling off five straight wins to end the regular season, averaging just shy of 40 points per game over the last month. The Giants were waiting again in the NFL title game, and again the Colts' defense was brilliant. They held the Giants to field goals again and again but still trailed 9-7 through three quarters. Unitas scored from four yards out to give the Colts the lead early in the fourth quarter, and a 42-yard interception by Johnny Sample pushed the lead to 28-9 as the team raced to a 31-16 win.

A decade later, Ewbank was with the AFL's New York Jets as they came of age and after four straight losing seasons went 8-5-1 in 1967, as Joe Namath threw for 4,007 yards and the team finished a game behind the Houston Oilers in the East Division. The next year, Ewbank guided the Jets to the East Division title at 11-3. They knocked off the Raiders 27-23 in the AFL title game and then shocked Baltimore 16-7 in the Super Bowl, making good on Namath's guarantee days earlier. The Jets went 10-4 the following year, winning the East again, but lost a 13-6 heartbreaker to the Chiefs in the AFL title game.

Lance Alworth

Lance Alworth was the first player who played primarily in the AFL to be elected to the Hall of Fame. At Arkansas, he was track star who dominated the 100 and 200-yard dashes along with the long jump. He was also a three-time Academic All-American with a degree in marketing on a pre-law bend. He was drafted by the 49ers in the NFL and the Raiders in the AFL. The Raiders traded his rights to the Chargers, and he moved from end to wide receiver. After a year on the bench, he exploded to franchise records of 61 receptions, 1,205 yards, and 11 touchdowns. Between 1964-1969, he kept on destroying franchise records and abusing league defenses. The previous record for most consecutive seasons of more than 1,000 yards receiving was three— Alworth did it for seven. In 1966, he led the league in five categories and had five different games of at least 200 yards receiving, still a record. His high-water mark came in 1965, when he compiled 1,602 yards receiving and 14 touchdowns. He is still 13th in yards receiving per game for his career.

Len Dawson

Len Dawson was drafted by the Pittsburgh Steelers in 1957 and spent three years with the Steelers, throwing exactly 17 passes for them. He then was sent to Cleveland where he spent two seasons and threw 28 passes. That's when Al Davis showed up. Davis had taken over as commissioner of the AFL, and the first thing he did was target talented quarterbacks who weren't getting their due in the NFL. Dawson signed with the Dallas Texans and was an immediate success, completing 61% of his passes for 2,759 yards and 29 touchdowns. The Texans moved to Kansas City the following year and Dawson never let up. He went 93-56-8 in his career for the Chiefs, which spanned until 1975. He led the league in completion percentage eight times and in touchdown passes four times. He led the Chiefs to titles in 1962, 1966, and 1969, and a Super Bowl win in Super Bowl IV, a game in which he was named the MVP.

He had suffered a nasty knee injury that year in the second game of the year and missed five games, only to return and lead the Chiefs to dramatic road playoff wins over the Jets and Raiders. By the end of his career, he was named to the all-time All-AFL team, the Chiefs Hall of Fame, and the Pro Football Hall of Fame. As big a fan of football as there ever was, Dawson served as host of the HBO's *Inside the NFL* from 1977 to 2001.

Don Maynard

Don Maynard's road to stardom was long and winding, and there were times when he felt like quitting or others felt like quitting for him. He attended thirteen schools growing up, as his father moved from place to place as a cotton broker. In college, he played a year for Rice and then three years for Texas Western. He caught just 28 passes in those three years, but ten of them were for touchdowns, and all told he averaged 27.6 yards per catch. Over the three years, he rushed for 843 yards on 154 attempts. The Giants took him with the 109th pick in the 1957 draft, and he played sparingly as a rookie before getting cut. He spent the 1958 season with the Hamilton Tiger-Cats of the

Canadian Football League, catching one pass the whole year.

When the AFL formed in 1960, New York Titans coach Sammy Baugh knew exactly who Maynard was, having seen him play in high school and college. He jumped on the chance despite critics calling him an NFL reject. He shut up every critic around by catching 72 passes for 1,265 yards and six touchdowns his first year. He put up 1,401 yards in 1962 but really came into his own in 1965 when the Jets added a rookie quarterback by the name of Joe Namath. Namath threw to Maynard 71 times in 1967, and Maynard racked up 1,434 yards—20.2 yards per catch and 102 yards per game with 10 touchdowns. The next year, he caught 57 passes for 1,297 yards and another 10 touchdowns. In the AFL title game, he caught six passes for 118 yards and two touchdowns, including the game winner. He suffered a bad hamstring injury in that game and did not play in the Jets' Super Bowl win over the Baltimore Colts. He is one of only 20 players to play all 10 years of the AFL's existence. He finished his career with 11,834 yards receiving and 88 touchdowns.

FACTS AND FIGURES

1. Before changing their name to the Raiders, the Oakland franchise was originally called the "Señores".

2. The Jets and Raiders combined for 850 total yards, 19 penalties, and 238 penalty yards during the Heidi game.

3. Joe Namath's rookie contract of $427,000 would be worth $3.36 million in today's dollars.

4. The first game called the Super Bowl was actually the third AFL-NFL title game.

5. The Jets were an 18-point underdog to the Colts in Super Bowl III.

6. In 1967, Joe Namath became the first rookie to throw for 4,000 yards in a season.

7. Between 1964 and 1966, Lance Alworth racked up 40 touchdown receptions.

8. Don Maynard and Art Powell were the first wide receiver tandem to go over 1,000 yards in the same season in 1960. They did it again in 1962.

9. Maynard's 18.7 yards per reception remains an NFL record for players with at least 600 career catches.

10. The 1969 Kansas Chiefs won two road playoff games to get to the Super Bowl.

11. The 1969 Chiefs allowed just 14 points in three postseason games en route to the Super Bowl crown.

12. Norm Van Brocklin was MVP in 1960 as the Philadelphia Eagles quarterback. It was his last year of playing pro football.

13. Oakland Raider kicker Larry Barnes was just 6 of 25 on field goals in 1960, going just 2-of-19 beyond 29 yards including a ghastly 1-of-12 from 30-39 yards.

14. The 1962 Oakland Raiders started the year 0-13 with nine of the losses coming by double digits. They upset the 9-3-1 Boston Patriots 20-0 to avoid a winless season.

15. The last-ever game played by the AFL was Super Bowl IV, a win by the Chiefs over the Vikings.

TRIVIA QUESTIONS

1. How many fans did the Raiders average during their first season in the AFL?

   A. 5,000

   B. 9,600

   C. 14,400

   D. 36,000

2. Who was the first AFL champion?

   A. Dallas

   B. Los Angeles

   C. Boston

   D. Houston

3. Who won the first AFL-NFL title game?

   A. Green Bay

   B. Chicago

   C. Houston

   D. Kansas City

4. Who did Don Maynard play for the year before signing with the New York Titans?

   A. The New York Giants

B. The Green Bay Packers

C. The Hamilton Tigers-Cats

D. No one

5. How many points were the Colts favored over the Jets in Super Bowl III?

A. 4

B. 8

C. 13

D. 18

Answers

1. B
2. D
3. A
4. C
5. D

CHAPTER 4

RISE OF THE SUPER TEAMS (1970S-1980S)

With new leagues forming and folding, and franchises doing likewise, it was hard for any team to maintain a level of consistent excellence through the early decades of the league. Once the AFL had merged with the NFL, however, things were stable for a good twenty years. This led to a number of franchises getting good and staying good, not just locking up great players and coaches but adopting identities and cultures that endure regime changes and player retirements. These squads permeated the existence of the fans' minds and became synonymous with certain ideals regardless of who was wearing the uniforms. These were the Super Teams of the 1970s and 1980s.

Dallas Cowboys (1966-1982, 2 Super Bowl Wins, 5 Super Bowl Appearances, 16 playoff appearances in 17 seasons).

Going to the playoffs 16 times in 17 years is how you become America's team. Having the same coach for all those years, and before and beyond too. Having a pair of all-time great quarterbacks didn't hurt either.

From 1966 to 1973, the Cowboys won eight straight division titles. Tom Landry had come on board at the start of the franchise in 1960 and gone winless, 0-11-1. The Cowboys finished below .500 every year until 1965, when they went 7-7 to finish second in the NFL East, overcoming a 2-5 start.

In 1967, the Cowboys exploded out of the gate to a 4-0-1 start, putting up 52 points on the Giants and 56 on the Eagles. They hammered Cleveland 52-14 in the divisional playoff round as Don Meredith was nearly perfect, completing 11 of 13 passes for 212 yards and 2 touchdowns. They missed out on taking the next step with a 21-17 loss at Green Bay in the conference title game when Bart Starr scored on a 1-yard touchdown run in the fourth quarter.

Dallas was one of the best teams in the regular season the following year, going 12-2 to win the Capitol Division. They finished first in the NFL in total offense and second in total defense. In Week 1, they clobbered the Lions 59-13 and started the year 6-0. They finished the year with five wins a row but were upset on the road at Cleveland in the first round of the playoffs despite beating the Browns easily earlier in the season. Meredith was just 3-of-9 for 42 yards with three interceptions before he was yanked for Craig Morton. At age 30, Meredith's days were starting to look numbered.

In 1969, the Cowboys went 11-2-1 as Meredith left, Morton took over as starter, and the team drafted a talented Navy grad named Roger Staubach. The Cowboys were shown the door again by their nemesis, Cleveland. The Browns trounced the Cowboys 42-10 in the regular season and 38-14 in the playoffs.

In 1970, the Cowboys finally escaped their own conference for the first time. Landry guided them to a 10-4 record in the NFC East behind a rigid defense that threw two regular-season shutouts and went on a stretch of three straight games allowing just five total points, including a watershed 6-2 road win at Cleveland. The Dallas defense held Cleveland to just 63 yards on the ground and forced four turnovers. That Defense served the Cowboy well in the playoffs, as they took an ugly 5-0 win over Detroit in the divisional playoffs. The defense held Detroit to 156 total yards and seven first downs. The next week they knocked off the San Francisco 49ers 17-10 in what would become a bitter postseason rivalry. Duane Thomas powered the offense with 143 yards rushing and a touchdown.

Dallas' first Super Bowl was a bitter pill to swallow, a 16-13 loss to the Colts at the Orange Bowl in which they led 13-6 at halftime and never scored again. The defense forced seven Colt turnovers, but Morton struggled with three interceptions of his own.

So close to their goal, the Cowboys took stock of what they had and what they needed, and Landry made a move. He replaced

Morton with Staubach as quarterback and the move paid off in spades. Staubach went 10-0 as a starter completing 59.7% of his passes for 1,882 yards, 15 touchdowns and just four interceptions.

Dallas finished the regular season on a 7-game winning streak and knocked off the Vikings on the road in the divisional playoffs on Christmas Day. The defense worked overtime, forcing five turnovers as the offense managed just 183 total yards. That set up a rematch with the 49ers in the title game. Dallas took the advantage again, 14-3, holding the 49ers to just nine first downs and intercepting their quarterback thrice.

Fresh blood awaited in the Super Bowl—another new Super Team in the making in the form of the Miami Dolphins. Dallas' defense as ample again, forcing three turnovers and limiting the Fish to ten first downs in 24-3 triumph. In a battle of future Hall of Famers, Roger Staubach outplayed Bob Griese by throwing for a pair of touchdowns.

Once established as a power, the Cowboys were in the mix for every title for years to come. In 1972, they went 10-4 in the regular season, won another thriller from the 49ers (30-28) in the divisional round, then were blasted 26-3 by the Redskins in the conference title game after sweeping them in the regular season. Calvin Hill became the feature of the offense, accounting for 1,400 yards and nine touchdowns. In 1973, it was another conference title appearance but a defeat at the hands of the Minnesota Vikings in the conference title game. Staubach took the quarterback job for good, throwing for 23 touchdowns.

The 1974 Cowboys were the only team not to make the playoffs in a 17-year span. They struggled early, losing four straight games to sit at 1-4, then won 6 of 7 before dropping the season finale to the Raiders. They returned to the playoffs despite losing the division in 1975, going 10-4. They ravaged the 1973 loss to Minnesota in the playoffs by chipping the Vikings at home 17-14 in the divisional round when Staubach heaved a 50-yard pass to new star Drew Pearson to win the game.

After struggling for years, Staubach suddenly had two killer weapons in Pearson and (no relation) Preston Pearson, who combined for nine catches for 168 yards against the Vikings. The defense was never better for the Cowboys than at that moment, led by Randy White, Mel Renfro, and Ed "Too Tall" Jones. In the NFC title game, the Cowboys thrashed the Rams 37-7 on the road, jumping out to a 34-0 lead as Staubach threw four touchdown passes in the first 2-3 quarters. Preston Pearson caught three of the scores and had 123 yards receiving for the game. Dallas nearly quadrupled Los Angeles in total yards, 441 to 118. That put Dallas back into the Super Bowl against the new rising force of the AFC—the Pittsburgh Steelers.

The Super Bowl played on January 18, 1976, at the Orange Bowl, was an all-time great. Ahead 10-7 at halftime, the Cowboys were beaten by a series of defensive standouts and a deep touchdown pass from Terry Bradshaw to Lynn Swann, losing 21-17. Pittsburgh's Steel Curtain defense swarmed Staubach for seven sacks, and he threw three interceptions. The Cowboys never got their rushing game going, leading them to pursue a new threat on the ground in the off-season. The Cowboys had a low draft pick but were willing to go all in on a difference maker. They found their window when Heisman Trophy winner Tony Dorsett told the Seattle Seahawks he didn't want to play for them. The Cowboys traded their #1 pick (#14 overall) and three second-round picks to the Seahawks to jump to the No. 2 pick in the 1977 draft.

Dorsett and Coach Landry didn't see eye to eye from the beginning, with Landry wanting to run set plays and Dorsett insisting he used his vision to find the holes. Eventually Landry gave in after watching his new star in action. It was the right move, as Dorsett rushed for 1,007 yards and scored 12 touchdowns his rookie year, dropping 206 yards on the Eagles in one game. In the divisional playoffs that year, Dorsett matched up against Walter Payton of the Chicago Bears. Dorsett had 85 yards and two touchdowns plus 37 yards receiving. Payton was held to 60 yards on 19 carries in a 37-7 Cowboys rout. The next week was a 16-6 victory over Minnesota in the NFC title game as the Cowboys rushed for 170 yards and two touchdowns as a team. Dorsett's addition gave the Cowboys exactly what they wanted—a return trip the Super Bowl and a second title, routing Denver 27-10. Dorsett scored the first touchdown of the game and running back Robert Newhouse threw a halfback pass for a

29-yard touchdown to make it 27-10.

The Cowboys made it back to the Super Bowl after the 1978 season, going 12-4. Dorsett ran for 1,325 yards and seven touchdowns, and Staubach, at age 36, was 11-4 as a starter with 3,190 yards and 25 touchdowns. After edging Atlanta 27-20 in the divisional round, the Cowboys humiliated the Rams 28-0 for the NFC title. The game was scoreless until the third quarter when Dorsett scored from five yards out. Linebacker Thomas Henderson capped the game for Dallas with a 68-yard interception return in the fourth quarter. Dallas' defense turned the Rams over seven times. That win led to a rematch with the Steelers in their Super Bowl. In one of the all-time great games, Pittsburgh prevailed 35-31 despite Dallas' success against the vaunted Steel Curtain defense. A dropped pass in the end zone by Jackie Smith is always remembered by Cowboys fans as the one that got away.

It would be the Cowboys last Super Bowl appearance for more than ten years. The next season, they went 11-5 but lost to the Rams 21-19 in the divisional round. In 1980, they finished second in the East to Philadelphia, then defeated the Rams and the Falcons on the road in the playoffs. Faced with a third shot at the Eagles, whom they had split two prior games with, the Cowboys' offense was stymied in a 20-7 loss. Staubach retired, and Danny White took over as quarterback, throwing for 3,287 yards and 28 touchdowns. Dorsett rushed for 1,185 yards and

11 scores. It marked the first of three straight title game losses for Dallas that ended its dynasty.

The 1981 season led to the famous Dwight Clark "The Catch" game against San Francisco in which the 49ers' wide receiver speared a six-yard loft from quarterback Joe Montana in the final seconds of a 28-27 Niners win in the NFC title game. Dallas finished second to Washington the following year—a strike-shortened season—then beat Tampa and Green Bay on the road in the playoffs for a rematch with the Skins. Down 14-3, the Cowboys got within 21-17 before losing 31-17.

Miami Dolphins (5 Super Bowls, 2 wins, 10 division titles, 1970-1985)

The Miami Dolphins were 3-10-1 in 1969—about as bad as you could get. They had a third-year quarterback named Bob Griese who threw 10 touchdowns and 16 interceptions, and a young fullback named Larry Csonka who had rushed for 566 yards in his first year. But things were about to change.

Don Shula, who had coached the Baltimore Colts to two Super Bowls, came on as the Dolphins head coach in 1970. After losing their season opener, the Dolphins ran off four wins in a row, and after losing three straight, ended the regular season with six straight wins. Griese became the full-time starter and threw for 2,019 yards. Csonka became the primary ball carrier and gained 874 yards while scoring six touchdowns.

The team made its first-ever playoff appearance, losing to the Raiders. What followed next was unprecedented in such a young franchise. Miami made it to three straight Super Bowls, winning two of them. After starting off the 1971 season 1-1-1, the Dolphins won eight straight games. Csonka ran for 1,051 yards and 7 touchdowns. In the layoffs, they edged Kansas City 27-24 in overtime then gave Shula one of the sweetest wins of his career, a 21-0 shutout of the Colts in the AFC title game. The Cinderella run ran out in the Super Bowl as the Dallas Cowboys dominated Miami to a 24-3 count.

The Dolphins were undaunted, aiming to be even better in 1972. What followed was the greatest single-season effort in league history. The Dolphins went 14-0—the only team in league history to that point to go without a defeat for a season. They finished first in team offense and team defense, more than doubling their opponents in scoring. Griese split time with Earl Morrall because of injuries, but the real power was the Dolphins' ground game. Csonka and Mercury Morris each topped 1,000 yards—Csonka had 1,117 and 6 touchdowns, Morris exactly 1,000 and 12 touchdowns.

The playoff games were all close, but at the same time, the Dolphins offense made all of them into simple exercises in ball-control domination. They trailed the Browns 14-13 in the fourth quarter of their divisional game before getting a late touchdown in a 20-14 win. The AFC title game was one of the best in history, with the Steelers hosting the Dolphins. The Dolphins ran the ball 49 times for 193 yards and only turned it over once. The Super Bowl was strength against strength. Washington ran the ball 36 times for 141 yards, Miami 37 times for 184 yards. The Dolphins won 14-7 and had their first Super Bowl title and the only perfect season in NFL history.

The Dolphins ran their win streak to 18 straight before losing the second week of the 1973 season. After a 12-7 loss to Oakland, they ran off 10 more games in a row, finishing the season 12-2. Csonka and Morris combined for 1,957 yards and 15 touchdowns, and Griese threw for 17 more.

The team rushed for 241 yards on 52 carries in defeating the Bengals in the divisional round, ten avenged their earlier loss to the Raiders with a 27-10 that saw Csonka score three touchdowns as the team ran for 266 yards on 53 carries. Griese only threw six passes in the game. The Vikings came calling for the Super Bowl in Houston, Texas, and never had a chance, held scoreless until the fourth quarter. Miami's rushing attack put up 196 yards and three touchdowns on 53 carries. Csonka was the runaway MVP with 145 yards and two touchdowns.

The Dolphins won another title the next year but lost in the first round of the playoffs. They won 10+ games in four of the next five seasons and made it back to the Super Bowl in the strike-shortened 1982 season. They lost to the Redskins, and the Csonka-Griese era was at an end, forcing Shula to reinvent how the Fins would win games. There were six quarterbacks projected for the first round of the NFL draft in 1983—Ken O'Brien, Tony Eason, Todd Blackledge, Dan Marino, Jim Kelly, and John Elway. Marino watched as one by one the players were chosen ahead of him. Marino had a weak senior season and was rumored to be on drugs. Marino was also drafted by the upstart USFL as the No. 1 pick, but he opted to go with the Dolphins. Backup to David Woodley, he was given his first start in Week 6 of the 1983 season.

Marino completed 19 of 29 passes for 322 yards and three touchdowns as the team lost in overtime 38-35 to Buffalo to fall to 3-3 on the year, but Marino had made believers out of his new bosses. He started the rest of the year and the Dolphins won 9 of their last 10 games to finish the regular season 1-4. He beat the Jets the next week by throwing for 225 yards and three touchdowns, and finished the regular season with 20 touchdowns against just six interceptions. The Dolphins were back in the playoffs but were upset 27-20 by Seattle as Marino completed just 15 of 25 passes.

With Marino's confidence growing, 1984 turned into one of the most cherished seasons in Miami history. Bringing back memories of the early 70s, the Dolphins won their first eleven games in a row and finished the regular season 14-2. Marino turned in a season for the ages, becoming the first quarterback to throw for 5,000 yards in a year (5,084) and tossing 48 touchdowns, shattering the previous record. Anyone watching knew things were going to be schedule from the get-go. Marino threw for 311 yards and five touchdowns in the season-opening win over the Redskins. In Week 5 against the Cardinals, he threw for 29 yards. The Jets were torched for 422 yards, the Patriots for 316 yards and 4 touchdowns. The Dolphins finally lost, 34-28 in overtime, at San Diego, but Marino threw two touchdowns and was 28-41 for 338 yards. In the other loss of the season, 45-34 to Oakland, he was 35-57 for 470 yards and four scores. For the year, he completed 64.2% of his passes and set the record for attempts (564) and completions (362).

In the playoffs, he threw three touchdowns in a 31-10 win over Seattle and four more in a 45-28 decimation of the Steelers. His two main targets were Mark Duper—the speedster, and Mark Clayton—the more reliable one. Clayton put together the greatest wide receiver season this side of Jerry Rice, catching 73 passes for 1,389 yards and 18 touchdowns. Duper caught 71 passes for 1304 yards and eight scores. There was just one chink in the armor—the San Francisco 49ers and their own incredible quarterback, Joe Montana. Playing in Stanford, basically a home game for the 49ers, who had gone 15-1 during the regular season, Montana outshone Marino in every facet of the game, throwing for 331 yards and three touchdowns and rushing for 59 yards and another score as San Francisco won 38-16.

The Dolphins went 12-4 the following year but had arguably the biggest regular-season win in NFL history. On Monday Night Football, the Dolphins beat the 11-0 Chicago Bears to ruin their bid at an undefeated season. Miami won the East and overcame a 21-3 deficit to beat the Browns in the divisional playoffs, putting them one win from a rematch with the Bears in Super Bowl XX. Instead, Miami was shocked 31-14 by New England, the Patriots first win in Miami since 1966. Marino went on to set nearly every passing record in NFL history, but the Dolphins never returned to the Super Bowl.

Pittsburgh Steelers (4 Super Bowl appearances, 4 wins, 7 division titles, 1972-1979)

For all of his grizzled looks and gruff demeanor, the one thing most people never realized about Pittsburgh head coach Chuck Noll was how utterly brilliant he drafted. In 1969, the new Steelers coach drafted Mean Joe Greene. In 1970, he selected Mel Blount and Terry Bradshaw, then Jack Ham in 1971 and Franco Harris in 1972. In 1974, he bettered that by taking Lynn Swann, Jack Lambert, John Stallworth, and Mike Webster in the same draft. This dynasty was grown at home.

Noll's first year, 1969, the team went 1-13. They improved to 5-9 in 1970 and 6-8 in 1971. It looked like another .500-ish year to start 1972 as the team went 2-2 out of the gate. But somewhere along the way, things started taking shape, especially on defense.

The Steelers ran off five straight wins, holding the Oilers to 7, the Patriots to 3, and the Chiefs to 7 in that stretch before losing to Cleveland by two. They won four more in a row to end the season, giving up a total of 15 points to the Vikings, Browns, Oilers, and Chargers to win the AFC Central with an 11-3 record.

Harris, in his first season, rushed for 1,055 yards and 10 touchdowns, averaging 5.6 yards per carry. Bradshaw threw for just 1,887 yards but tossed 12 touchdown passes and was an impressive runner in his own right, averaging more than 20 yards a game rushing and scoring seven touchdowns. But it was the Steel Curtain defense that made things glorious. The Steelers had 28 interceptions and 31 fumble recoveries—59 turnovers forced in just 14 games. Linebacker Jack Ham had seven interceptions, Mike Wagner had six, John Rowser four, and Mel Blount 3. In their 30-0 rout of the Browns, they held Cleveland's offense to 126 yards. Houston had 159 the next week, San Diego 172 the week after that.

Their divisional playoff with Oakland was their first playoff game since 1947. It was 7-6 Raiders into the fourth quarter until the play echoed around the world as the Immaculate Reception. It was 4th and 10 at Pittsburgh's own 40 with 22 seconds to play when Jack Tatum hit Bradshaw's arm as he tried to throw a deep pass. Harris, downfield to block, collected the battered pass as it wobbled end over end, scooping it up before it hit the turf and running 60 yards for the go-ahead touchdowns. Steeler fans stormed the field, and it took 15 minutes to clear it so Pittsburgh could kick the extra point for the tally. The Steelers moved on, the Raiders went home, and a fearsome rivalry was born. The play made up nearly one-third of the Steelers' passing yardage for the game. The Steel Curtain defense was unbelievable, holding the Raiders to 102 yards passing on just 12 of 30 with two interceptions. Harris was the game's star, with 160 yards of total offense.

On its way to an undefeated season, Miami held off Pittsburgh 21-17 in the AFC title game, but the Steelers had made a name for themselves at long last. They went 10-3 the following year only to lose in the divisional playoffs to the Raiders, 33-14. The next season, Pittsburgh went 10-3-1 in the regular season. The defense allowed just 13.5 points per game, starting the season 1-1-1. The Steelers ran off five wins in a row and reached the postseason at 10-3-1 having thrown two shutouts and limited three other opponents to seven points or less. In the playoffs, they erupted for 26 points in the second period to beat Buffalo 32-14, then stunned the hated Raiders in Oakland. Trailing 10-3 after three quarters, the Steelers got two Harris touchdown runs and a pass from Bradshaw to Lynn Swann to take a 24-13 win and reach their first Super Bowl. The Steel Curtain was amazing against Minnesota, allowing the Vikings 119 yards total and just 17 on the ground. They intercepted Fran Tarkenton three times, and Harris rushed 34 times for 158 yards and a touchdown. Pittsburgh was atop the football world.

With their winning formula locked in, Pittsburgh now went forward to conquer the football world twice in a row. After an ugly 30-21 loss to Buffalo early in the year, they began one of the greatest defensive seasons of all time. In 14 regular season games, the Steelers allowed less than 12 points per game, holding eight opponents to 10 points or less. The defense produced 48 turnovers and 43 sacks. Mel Blount recorded 11 interceptions for 121 yards. On the ground, Harris pounded defenses for 1,246 yards and 10 touchdowns. Bradshaw threw 18 touchdowns, and Swann caught 11 of them. In the playoffs, Harris ran for 153 yards and a touchdown against the Colts, and another showdown with the Raiders produced a 16-10 Steelers' win as 23 of the game's 26 points game in the fourth quarter. The Steelers overcame seven turnovers. Battling Dallas for the Super Bowl title, a gorgeous 64-yard pass from Bradshaw made it a 21-10 lead late. The Steel Curtain rattled Roger Staubach into three fumbles and three interceptions. The Steelers won 21-17 for back-to-back titles.

Another 10-4 season gave them hopes of a third straight title, but Oakland beat them 24-7 in the conference championship. After a 9-5 season led to an early playoff loss, the Steelers refocused for their best purpose. Their 1978 campaign saw them score 356 points and allow just 195 while putting together a 14-2 record. They started the season 7-0, keeping four opponents to 10 points or fewer. Their first loss was a big surprise, the upstart Houston Oilers, led by rookie running back sensation Earl Campbell, knocked off the Steelers 24-17. After falling 10-7 to the Rams two weeks later, the Steelers won their next five games, including knocking off the Oilers, 13-3, to take the division title.

In the playoffs, Pittsburgh steamrolled Denver and Houston by a combined 68-15 score. Against Houston in the AFC title game, Pittsburgh recorded a staggering 9 turnovers in a rainy day at Three Rivers Stadium, intercepting Dan Pastorini five times and pouncing on three Campbell fumbles.

The Super Bowl was a marvelous shootout that saw the Steelers beat the Cowboys 35-31, trailing just once 14-7 before Bradshaw found John Stallworth for a 75-yard touchdown. It was the postseason highlight of Bradshaw's career as he threw for 318 yards and 4 touchdowns. The Steelers enjoyed the best offense in the league in 1979, averaging 26 points per game. Bradshaw threw for 3,274 yards and 26 touchdowns, and Harris rushed for 1,186. In the playoffs, they dropped 20 points on the Dolphins in the first quarter of a 34-14 win, then rallied past Houston 10-3 in the AFC title game rematch. The Rams had upset the Cowboys in the NFC title game and led Pittsburgh 13-10 at halftime of the Super Bowl before the champs charged back, scoring 21 of the next 27 points to repeat as champions.

It would mark the end of the Steelers' era. Beaten down by age and injury in 1980, they finished behind both Houston and Cleveland, finishing 9-7 and missing the postseason. They would not return to the Super Bowl for 16 years and wouldn't win another one until 2005.

Oakland Raiders (4 Super Bowl appearances, 3 Super Bowl wins, 12 division titles, 1967-1985)

Their Super Bowl wins were a bit more spread out than some other Super Teams, but Oakland's sheer longevity of prowess is hard to top. The Raiders had one losing season, and that a 7-9 one, between 1965 and 1986, winning three Super Bowls under three different coaches. After two straight years with winning records but no playoffs to show for it, the Raiders went 13-1 in 1967, representing the AFL in the second-ever Super Bowl. A week four loss to the New York Jets was all that had kept the Raiders from an undefeated season, and its offense had been impressive all year, topping 50 points twice. Oakland was the rare "throw first" team in the 1960s, with Daryle Lamonica tossing 30 touchdowns on 220-of-425 attempts for 3,228 yards. Former No. 1 pick Billy Cannon had converted from running back to tight end and racked up 629 yards receiving and 10 touchdowns. And the Raiders had secret weapon George Blanda, the 40-year-old place kicker who boomed 20 field goals on the year and hit on 56 of 57 extra points.

In the AFL title game, the Raiders ran over the Houston Oilers 40-7, rushing for 263 yards and holding the Oilers to just 38 yards on the ground. The Super Bowl was a horse of a different color as the Packers forced three Oakland turnovers and rolled to a 33-14 victory.

Oakland's quest to avenge that loss took some time, though not for lack of effort. The Raiders made it to the conference title game in each of the next three seasons, putting up a combined record of 32-7-3 in the process. In 1968, it was a narrow defeat to the New York Jets, 27-23, that ended the Raiders season and demanded a coaching change, with a 32-year-old named John Madden coming on the scene for the 1969 season.

Madden had never played pro ball because of a knee injury but had risen quickly through the coaching ranks, serving under offensive whiz Don Coryell at San Diego State before coming on board with the Raiders as their linebacker's coach. He took over as the head man in 1969 and went 12-1-1 before losing to the eventual Super Bowl champion Kansas City. Between 1969 and 1975, the Raiders made the conference title game four times and lost all four. LaMonica was quarterback until 1972, but a sub-par year saw Madden turn to his former No. 1 draft pick Ken Stabler, who had sitting the bench behind LaMonica for years.

Stabler threw for just shy of 2,000 yards and 14 touchdowns in his first season in charge and was named to the Pro Bowl. He got better and better, guiding the Raiders to a 23-5 record over the next two years, throwing for 2,469 yards and 26 touchdowns in 1974, but losing the AFC title game both years to the Pittsburgh Steelers, who won back-to-back Super Bowls. Finally, in 1976, the Raiders put it all together. After being humiliated 48-17 by New England in week 4, the team won 10 straight games to end the regular season. Stabler tossed 27 touchdown passes in 11 games, and fullback Mark van Eeghen carried the ball 233 times for 1,012 yards, while stud receiver Cliff Branch hauled in 46 passes for a whopping 1,111 yards and 12 touchdowns. Tight end Dave Casper caught 10 touchdowns.

The Raiders exorcised long and short-term demons in the playoffs. In the divisional round, they took out the Patriot team that had trounced them earlier, overcoming a 21-10 fourth-quarter deficit with two short rushing touchdowns to take a 24-21 win. In the title game, the Raiders manhandled the Pittsburgh Steelers 24-7, holding Pittsburgh scoreless for three of the four quarters. Franco Harris missed the game injured, and the Steelers were held to 72 yards rushing while Terry Bradshaw completed just 14 of 35 passes. The Raiders played smash mouth football all game, rushing the ball 51 times for 157 yards to reach the Super Bowl.

After a scoreless first quarter, Oakland blitzed the Minnesota Vikings for 16 second-quarter points and never looked back, cruising to a 32-14 victory that was punctuated by Willie Brown's 75-yard interception return in the fourth quarter. Oakland ran the ball 52 times for 266 yards, led by Clarence Davis' 16 carries for 137 yards.

The Raiders continued to win games over the next three years, but without postseason success. They lost the conference title game in 1977, then went 9-7 the next two years and missed the playoffs entirely. In 1980, the Raiders made NFL history, becoming the wildcard team to advance to the Super Bowl and win it. Doing this meant winning a wildcard game at home and then two games on the road to make the Super Bowl. But that's putting the cart in front of the horse.

After two straight 9-7 seasons, Al Davis was done with the current lineup and wanted a change. He succeeded in a blockbuster trade, sending Stabler to the Houston Oilers for quarterback Dan Pastorini, who had guided Houston to back-to-back AFC title game losses to Pittsburgh. A native of Sonora, Pastorini had gone to college at Santa Clara and had been the Oilers quarterback since 1971. With Pastorini at the helm, the Raiders split their first four games, losing to rival San Diego in overtime and getting hammered 24-7 by the Buffalo Bills on the road. The next week against the Kansas City Chiefs, Pastorini was hit hard while scrambling and broke his leg, rendering him out for the season. Jim Plunkett, who was drafted the same year as Pastorini from nearby Stanford entered the game and threw for 238 yards and two touchdowns, but also five interceptions. The Raiders had fallen behind the Chiefs 31-0 and lost 31-17.

The next week offered a rematch with the Chargers, who were already 5-0 and looking to take complete command of the AFC West. San Diego piled up 435 yards of offense, but the Raider defense turned the ball over six times, leading to a shocking 38-24 Oakland win. Kenny King ran for 138 yards and two touchdowns, and Plunkett's precision passing—11 of 14 for 164 yards and a touchdown—was exactly what Oakland needed. The Chargers rallied to tie the game at 24 in the fourth quarter, but King took a pitch and went 89 yards to the house with it, and Todd Christensen recovered a San Diego in the end zone to slam the door and put Oakland back in the playoff picture.

The Raiders won their next six games in a row, including a 45-34 trashing of Pittsburgh that was the unofficial burial marker of the once mighty Steel Curtain defense. The Raiders only lost two games the rest of the way, both narrow contests to NFC contenders—10-7 to the Philadelphia Eagles and 19-13 to the Dallas Cowboys. Plunkett went 9-2 as a starter, throwing 18 touchdown passes. The Raider defense was led by the unstoppable force known as Lester Hayes, who intercepted 13 passes, the second-most in league history.

Finishing 11-5, Oakland was a game behind division champion San Diego, which meant they would have to win three times to reach the Super Bowl. As fate would have it, the other wildcard team that year in the AFC was the Houston Oilers, whom Stabler had helped to an 11-5 record as well.

The game was nip-and-tuck throughout the first half, with Earl Campbell scoring for Houston and Plunkett tossing a 1-yard touchdown pass to Todd Christensen to give the Raiders a 10-7 lead at intermission. It remained that way into the fourth quarter when the Raiders put up 17 points, the final seven on a Hayes' interception return for a touchdown, to take a 27-7 triumph.

The next week sent the Raiders to Cleveland for a division game where the temperature at kickoff was 4 degrees. In the brutal conditions, mistakes were plentiful and missed field goals and fumbles abound. The Raiders led 7-6 at halftime but trailed 12-7 entering the fourth quarter. An 80-yard drive early in the fourth quarter got the Raiders in front 14-12. The Raiders had a third and 1 at the Cleveland 15 on their next drive but had missed multiple field goals and tried to run the ball. They failed, and the Browns took over on downs. Quarterback Brian Sipe found his touch, hitting Ozzie Newsome for 29 yards and Greg Pruitt for 23. Pruitt had a 14-yard rush to the Raiders 14 and another short gain to the 13. Cleveland called timeout with 49 seconds to play, with the option of being conservative to set up a short field goal to win the game. However, kicker Don Cockroft had missed two field goals already, had an extra point blocked, and another never happened in a bad snap.

The Browns decided to try for a touchdown first, and Sipe ran a play called Red Slot Right, Halfback Stay, 88, designed to go to All-Pro tight end Newsome. Browns head coach Sam Rutigliano told Sipe to throw the ball into Lake Erie if the play wasn't open. Sipe believed he could make the throw and forced it to Newsome, but Raider safety Mike Davis stepped in front and intercepted it, sealing the Raiders win. The victory set up a showdown with the Chargers in San Diego for the AFC title. Although the final score was 34-27 Raiders, the game was decided quickly as Oakland led 21-7 in the first quarter and 28-14 at halftime. Chargers quarterback Dan Fouts threw for 336 yards and two touchdowns, but it took him 45 attempts to get there, and he was picked off twice. Plunkett was the model of consistency, 14-of-18 for 261 yards and 2 touchdowns, a quarterback rating of 155.8. Lester Hayes recorded yet another interception for the Oakland defense.

The Raiders were back in the Super Bowl for the first time in four years, and again they ran away from their opponents early. Plunkett found Cliff Branch for two touchdowns of 2 and 29 yards and a swing pass to Kenny King went for an 80-yard touchdown. It was 14-3 at halftime and 24-3 before the Eagles scored a touchdown in the fourth quarter. Oakland won 27-10, holding the Eagles to a mere 69 yards rushing and forcing four turnovers.

Three years later, they would win it all again, guided by the 36-year-old Plunkett and a remarkable young talent at running back named Marcus Allen, the pride of USC.

The Heisman Trophy-winning Allen rushed for 1,014 yards and 9 touchdowns and caught 68 passes for another 590 yards. Tight end Todd Christensen had one of the best seasons ever by a big man, grabbing 92 receptions for 1,247 yards and 12 touchdowns. The Raiders defense was swarming, sacking opposing quarterbacks 57 times, and racking up 53 takeaways (33 fumble recoveries, 20 interceptions). Their playoff run was one of the most dominating in league history as they outscored the Steelers, Seahawks, and Redskins by a 106-33 margin, averaging 399 yards of total offense per game. They beat Pittsburgh 38-10. Falling behind 3-0, the Raiders scored 31 unanswered points with two Allen touchdown runs and a Lester Hayes interception return for a touchdown. Allen rushed for 121 yards on just 13 carries in the win.

In the AFC title game, the Raiders put Seattle in a 20-0 hole at halftime and never let them out of it. Frank Hawkins rushed for two short touchdowns early on. Allen piled up 154 yards on 25 carries, and added seven catches for 62 yards and a score.

The Super Bowl was same song, third verse. Oakland led 21-3 at halftime with a defensive and special teams touchdown. After Washington got within 21-9, Allen scored on runs of 5 and 74 yards, and Chris Bahr added a 38-yard field goal for the 38-9 final score. Allen set a still-standing Super Bowl record with 191 yards on 20 carries, adding 18 yards receiving to reach 209 total yards. The Raiders defense sacked Joe Theismann six times and picked off two of his passes.

Washington Redskins (4 Super Bowl appearances, 3 wins, 5 divisional titles, 1982-1991)

Nobody liked the strike year of 1982 more than the Washington Redskins. The team had gone 14-18 the previous two years and hadn't been to the playoffs since 1976. They were 2-0 when the strike took place and won 6 of 7 games after it concluded, losing only to arch-rival Dallas to finish the shortened season 8-1. With a round-robin playoff system in action, everyone had to play three playoff games if they were to reach the Super Bowl. The Redskins were led by two "old-timers—33-year-old players Joe Theismann and John Riggins. Theismann threw for 2,033 yards and 13 touchdowns, while Riggins ran for 553 yards. Young receiver Charlie Brown had come on and electrified the city with 690 yards and eight touchdowns in nine games, and kicker Mark Moseley was so amazing that he won the league MVP, hitting 20 of 21 field goals and 16 of 19 extra points. As the top seed in the postseason, Washington got all three of its games at home and it paid off.

Theismann hit Alvin Garrett for 3 straight touchdown passes in the wildcard as the Redskins blasted Detroit 31-7. Riggins rushed for 119 yards, and Theismann was 14 of 19 for 210 yards in the easy win. The following week, the Redskins pounced early on Minnesota for a 14-0 first quarter lead. Both teams added a touchdown in the second quarter, and that was it; a scoreless second half led to a 21-7 Washington win. The Redskins played ball control to the extreme as Riggins rushed for a team record 37 attempts, racking up 185 yards and a touchdown. The NFC title game saw the Redskins hosting hated rival Dallas. Theismann and Riggins combined for the early scoring, but Dallas crept within 21-7 in the third quarter. Mosley's 29-yard field goal pushed the Washington lead to seven, and Darryl Grants late interception return made it a two-score lead. Washington won 31-17 as Riggins again was relentless with 36 carries for 140 yards and two scores.

In the Super Bowl, Riggins was dominant gain, rushing 38 times for 166 yards and a touchdown. The defense held Miami to nine first downs and 97 yards passing, forcing two turnovers. The Dolphins led 17-10 after a kickoff return for a touchdown, but Washington outscored Miami 17-0 after halftime, with Riggins' 43-yard touchdown run putting them ahead to stay. Riggins' four-game, postseason stretch remains arguably the single greatest postseason performance in NFL history. The Diesel left it all on the field for his team.

The Redskins went 14-2 the next year, clearly the pride of the NFC, but were manhandled 38-9 in the Super Bowl by the Oakland Raiders. They led the league in scoring at 33.8 points per game and put up a record 51 in the divisional round against the Los Angeles Rams. At age 34, Riggins rushed for 1,347 yards and 24 touchdowns on 375 carries. Charlie Brown had a career year receiving with 78 grabs or 1,225 yards and eight touchdowns. On defense, a rookie named Darrell Green made 109 tackles from his cornerback position.

Theismann and Riggins would ride off into the sunset a few years later, but the Skins stayed strong, winning double digit games the next three years, and losing the conference championship in 1986. 1987 saw a 15-game season with three games played strictly by scab players during another NFL strike. The Skins benefited greatly from that stretch, with their scabs winning all three games, two against divisional opponents. For the year, the team went 11-4 to win the NFC East. Jay Schroeder went 8-2 as the starting quarterback, and George Rogers led the team in rushing. It was running back by committee as at least six players eclipsed 100 yards rushing on the year. On defense, Barry Wilburn had 9 interceptions, including a 100-yarder for a touchdown, and Charles Mann led the line with 9.5 sacks and 80 tackles. Dexter Manley, who would later become the face of the NFL's drug problem, had 8.5 sacks.

The Skins barely escaped their first two playoff games, the first at Soldier Field. Schroeder had been hurt in the regular season, leaving Doug Williams to take over as quarterback. Williams had been the first-round draft pick of the Buccaneers in 1978 and one of the only black quarterbacks in the league. He had gone 33-33-1 in five years as the Bucks' starter and come in relief when Schroeder went down against Minnesota at the end of the year, throwing for 217 yards and two scores.

Down 14-0 in the second quarter to the Bears, they scored three straight touchdowns, the go-ahead on a 52-yard punt return by Green. They held the Bears to a single field goal in the second half. The Vikings upset San Francisco in the other divisional game, meaning Washington got to host the NFC title game. Williams completed just 9 passes but 2 were for touchdowns. The second was to Gary Clark in the fourth quarter of the gritty 17-10 lead.

Washington's shaky play made them the underdog against the AFC champion Broncos and the great John Elway, and that looked like the case as Denver took a 10-0 first quarter lead. What followed were perhaps the 15 most unlikely minutes in Super Bowl history.

On the Redskins first play of the second quarter, Williams hit Ricky Sanders for an 80-yard touchdown pass to make it 10-7. Denver went 3 and out to punt, and the Redskins began feeding running back Timmy Smith. A sporadic starter throughout the year who drew the lion's share of carries in the Super Bowl, had a 19-yard gainer to set up a 27-yard touchdown pass from Williams to Gary Clark, putting the Redskins up 14-10. The Broncos then drove to the Washington 26 before missing a field goal. Two plays later, Smith went 58 yards to the house. Eight minutes had gone by in the second quarter, and the Redskins had scored 21 points.

Elway and company went three-and-out, and Washington took

over on its own 40. Three plays later, Williams hit Sanders on a 50-yard bomb to make it 28-10 and the four minute mark. Elway was then intercepted by Barry Wilburn, and Williams hit Clint Didier for an 8-yard score with 1:11 to play in make it 35-10. Brian Davis intercepted Elway again with 7 seconds left in the first half. It was the most shocking turn of events in Super Bowl history, and the Redskins cruised to a 42-10 win. Elway threw three interceptions and was sacked five times. Williams threw for 340 yards and 4 touchdowns, and Smith ran for a Super Bowl record 204 yards and two touchdowns on 22 carries. Ricky Sanders caught 9 passes for 193 yards and two touchdowns.

Four years later, the Redskins had one last hurrah. After consecutive 10-6 seasons, they gave Joe Gibbs one last thrill by putting together a 14-2 regular season to win the NFC East. They went 11-0 to start the season, including two shutouts and seven games in which they scored at least 30 points. They wound up 14-2, resting many starters in a season-ending loss to Philadelphia. In the divisional round of the playoffs, they put the defensive clamps on the Atlanta Falcons, 24-7, then blitzed Detroit 41-10 in the conference title game. Mark Rypien had taken over for Williams at quarterback, but it was the rushing attack and defense doing the work against the Falcons as Ricky Ervins piled up 104 yards and touchdown.

Against Detroit, the Washington defense bottled up Barry Sanders to just 44 yards while Mark Rypien completed 12 of 17 passes for 228 yards and two scores. Detroit turned the ball over three times, Washington none.

In the Super Bowl, the Redskins made short work of the Buffalo Bills, en route to their second of four straight Super Bowl losses. Gerald Riggs scored two touchdowns as Washington led 17-0 at halftime and 24-0 before the Bills got on the board. Buffalo never got closer than the final margin of victory, 37-24, as Washington's defense held the Bills to 43 yards rushing. Jim Kelly was sacked five times and threw four interceptions, while Rypien was 18 of 33 for 292 yards and two scores. Gary Clark (114) and Art Monk (113) both topped 100 yards receiving.

San Francisco 49ers (4 Super Bowl appearances, 4 wins, 8 division titles, 1981-1990)

Bill Walsh did little to establish himself in his first two years as head coach of the San Francisco 49ers. The team went 2-14 in 1979 and 6-10 in 1980.They weren't the laughing stock of the league in 1980, because they were in the same division as the Saints, who went 1-15. In 1979, the team took a rookie quarterback out of Notre Dame in the draft, and in 1981, Walsh felt he had put in enough work to release Steve DeBerg in favor of Joe Montana, then 25.

The 49ers lost two of their first three games to no one's surprise, but then things started happening. They won six straight games, including a 45-14 demolition of Dallas that had heads turning as Montana threw for 279 yards and two touchdowns, and the Cowboys couldn't move the ball to save their lives, turning it over four times. A 15-12 loss to Cleveland was the only blemish on San Francisco's schedule the rest of the year, and they entered the playoffs 13-3 as the No. 1 seed.

Their first playoff game in nine years was a Montana celebration as he threw two touchdown passes and completed 20 of 31 passes for 304 yards. He threw six of those to Freddie Solomon, who had 107 yards and a touchdown, and another five to Dwight Clark for 104 yards. The Niners defense turned New York over four times, the most dramatic being Ronnie Lott's 20-yard interception return to put the game on ice. San Fran won 38-24.

That set up a rematch with the Cowboys that would go down as one of the greatest games in postseason history. Six turnovers kept the Niners from running away with the win, and Dallas, a 3-point favorite, took a 27-21 lead late on a Danny White touchdown pass. Undaunted, Montana led the team down the field and found Dwight Clark in the back of the end zone with seconds to play to seal a 28-27 win. Clark caught 8 passes for 120 yards and two touchdowns. In the Super Bowl, Montana matched up against Ken Anderson, the veteran leader of the Cincinnati Bengals. Both teams were in their first Super Bowl, but the Niners looked like old pros in racing out to a 20-0 lead as Montana threw one touchdown and rushed for another. The Bengals crept within

102

20-14 at the beginning of the fourth quarter, but Ray Wersching's two field goals salted the game away.

The Niners lost the 1983 NFC title game to Washington then put together the best season at that time in 1984, going 15-1 in the regular season. They were #1 in defense and #2 in offense. The 49ers raced out to a 6-0 record before losing to Pittsburg by a field goal. They bounced back with nine wins in a row, scoring more than 30 points 10 times, including 51 against the Vikings in week 15. Montana was brilliant, completing 64.6% of his passes for 28 touchdowns and 3,630 yards. Fullback Roger Craig was dynamic as a runner and receiver, piling up 1,325 yards and 10 touchdowns. The Niners allowed just 10 points in their two playoff wins, beating a tough Giants team 21-10 before shutting out the Bears 23-0. Montana was 25 of 39 for 309 yards and 3 touchdowns against New York, and the defense held Chicago to 13 first downs and 186 total yards in the NFC title game.

The Super Bowl was the most premiere quarterback matchup in decades. Miami's record-setting Dan Marino had no help from his rushing attack, however, and completed 29 of 50 passes for 318 yards and a touchdown, but was intercepted twice, lost a fumble, and sacked four times. Montana only got sacked once as he went 24 of 35 for 331 yards and a trio of touchdowns in the 38-16 win.

The 49ers watched as the Bears, Giants, and Redskins took the next three Super Bowls. Montana suffered a severe back injury in 1986 during the first week of the season, and doctors suggested he retire, but he came back that year and helped the team go 10-5-1. The 49ers trade for Tampa quarterback Steve Young was an insurance policy, and Young played well enough to create a quarterback controversy. The years without a Super Bowl were only made tolerable by the grandeur at wide receiver—Jerry Rice. Drafted in 1985, Rice caught 49 balls for 927 yards in his rookie year, starting four games. He started every game possible for next 18 years.

In 1986, he led the league with 1,570 yards and 15 touchdowns, and set a wide receiver record with 22 touchdown grabs in 1987. He reached 1,000 yards receiving for the next 11 seasons and had fewer than 10 touchdowns only once (9 in 1988). In 1995, he set a record for receiving yards in a season with 1,848.

In 1988, Montana went 8-5 as a starter and Young 2-1. The team won the NFC West with a 10-6 record and caught fire in the playoffs. Minnesota was whipped 34-9 and the Bears 28-3 to get the 49ers back to a Super Bowl, seeing Cincinnati again, a rematch of their 1981 clash. The 49ers weapons were legion: Roger Craig had gained 2,036 all-purpose yards with 1,502 on the ground and 10 total touchdowns, while Rice caught 64 passes for 1,306 yards. The Bengals, behind Boomer Esiason, led 13-6 after three quarters before Montana found Rice to tie things up. The Bengals went ahead on a field goal, but Montana drove the Niners down the field and hit John Taylor for a 10-yard touchdown with a minute to play, locking up a 20-16 win.

Walsh retired, and George Seifert took over as the head coach with the most weapons in the league. It showed the following year. Montana started 13 games and went 11-2 with 26 touchdowns against only eight interceptions and threw for 3,521 yards. Craig had 1,527 all-purpose yards and seven touchdowns, and Rice caught 82 passes for 1,483 yards and 17 scores. During the regular season, the 49ers lost to the Rams by one point and the Packers by four points. Otherwise, they were perfect, finishing first in scoring and third in defense. Their postseason run was like a victory parade onto itself. In the divisional round, Montana had four touchdown passes in the first half, and Rice finished the game with six catches for 114 yards and two touchdowns as they blasted the Vikings 41-13.

That led to a matchup with the Rams, who had scored one of two wins against San Francisco that year. Up 3-0 after a quarter, the Rams never scored again in a 30-3 loss. The Niners defense held the Rams to nine first downs and 156 yards, intercepting Jim Everett three times. Jonathan was near perfect, completing 26 of 30 passes for 262 yards and two touchdowns.

The Super Bowl matched Montana against John Elway, whose Broncos entered the game 13-5. What followed was the biggest rout in Super Bowl history as San Francisco scored in double digits in all four quarters for a 55-10 blowout. Rice, perhaps the greatest player the game has ever seen regardless of position, caught seven passes for 148 yards and three touchdowns. Montana was 22 of 29 for 297 yards and 5 scores.

Elway was smothered all game long, finishing 10 of 26 for 108 yards with no touchdowns, two interceptions and, 4 sacks. The 49er repeat was real.

1985 Chicago Bears

They only won one Super Bowl, and wouldn't make it back for another for 21 years, but the 1985 Chicago Bears are remembered as perhaps the greatest team in the modern history of the NFL. They had gone 10-6 the year before losing the NFC title game in San Francisco. Head coach Mike Ditka had played professionally for the Bears and Cowboys and was a tough SOB with a ton of attitude. Defensive coordinator Buddy Ryan was among the greatest teachers of the game ever. The team was blessed with a ferocious defense, giant offensive line, the greatest running back of all time from a purity standpoint, and a hotdog quarterback whose character made him a pop culture figure even 30 years later. The Bears gave up more than 20 points in two of their first three games, but won both of them. They gave up more than 19 just once the rest of the season, and during a stretch from October 13 to November 24, allowed an average of seven points per game over a seven-game stretch. The defense was led by Pro Bowlers Richard Dent, Steve McMichael, Otis Wilson, Dan Hampton, Dave Duerson, Mike

Singletary, and Wilber Marshall. Dent had 17 sacks and Wilson 10.5. The Bears intercepted 34 passes and recovered 27 fumbles—61 takeaways in a 16-game season. They racked up 46 sacks as well. Eight different players had at least two interceptions. Kick returner Willie Gault averaged 26.2 yards per kickoff return. Kevin Butler nailed all 51 of these extra points and 31 out of 37 field goals, going 28-of-29 inside 40 yards.

Jim McMahon missed five games to injury, but he was 11-0 as a starter, completing 57% of his throws. Walter Payton rushed for 1,551 yards and caught 49 passes for another 483 yards, good for 2,034 all-purpose yards. Gault caught 33 passes for 704 yards. And a 300-pound defensive lineman named William "The Refrigerator" Perry, carried the ball five times for seven yards and two touchdowns, and caught a 4-yard pass for a score, becoming America's favorite big man overnight.

In the divisional playoffs, the Bears blanked the Giants 21-0. The Giants had 181 yards of total offense and 10 first downs. The next week they blanked the Rams 24-0 in the NC title game. The Rams had 130 yards of total offense. All-Pro running back Eric Dickerson was held to 46 yards on 17 carries. The Bears had expected to play the Miami Dolphins, the only team to beat them in the regular season, again in the Super Bowl. But the New England Patriots stunned Miami 31-14.

Other than scoring first, the Patriots barely registered a pulse in the Super Bowl. Down 3-0, the Bears scored the next 44 points of the game, with McMahon rushing for two touchdowns, Perry for another, and Reggie Phillips returning an interception 28 yards for a touchdown. The patriots turned the ball over six times, fumbling four times. Steve Grogan was sacked four times, the last for a safety. Chicago held the ball for more than 39 minutes. When the game was over, both Ditka and Ryan were carried off the field by the players as the Bears won 46-10.

Earl Campbell and Luv Ya Blue

By the time the Houston Oilers reached their first AFC title game, the Dallas Cowboys had already played in four Super Bowls and won two of them. Houston was the little brother in Texas without even having a chance. After winning the first two AFL titles, the Oilers had been terrible. They didn't make the playoffs at all between 1969 and 1977, with only two winning seasons to show for. That all changed when owner Bud Adams convinced the Buccaneers to trade him the #1 draft pick, allowing them to take Earl Campbell, the 1977 Heisman Trophy winner from the University of Texas. Campbell was the ultimate combination of power and seed, and he became the first NFL rookie to win MVP honors when he carried the ball for 1,450 yards and 13 touchdowns in 1978, helping the Oilers to a 10-6 record and a playoff berth. Campbell rushed for 137 yards and a touchdown in his first game, and had seven games over 100 yards as a rookie. The greatest was when the Oilers hosted the Miami Dolphins in late November on Monday Night Football. Campbell carried the ball 28 times for 199 yards and four touchdowns, the last an 81-yard sprint to put the game out of reach. The Oilers won 35-30.

They saw the Dolphins again in the 1978 wildcard game and shocked Miami at home 17-9 on Christmas Eve. Oilers quarterback Dan Pastorini threw for 306 yards and a touchdown, completely outclassing Bob Griese, and Campbell's 1-yard touchdown run sealed the win. The next week, the Oilers took to Foxboro to take on the New England Patriots. Scoreless after a quarter, the Oilers rang up 21 points on three Pastorini touchdown passes, two to tight end Mike Barber. When the Patriots pulled within 24-14, Campbell scored a touchdown to make it 31-14. Campbell ran 27 times for 118 yards and a touchdown.

That set up a tilt between the Oilers and Pittsburgh Steelers. On a rainy day in Three Rivers Stadium, Houston was dismantled 34-5, turning the ball over nine times.

With good old boy coach Bum Phillips, who wore a cowboy hat to all road games but took it off inside the Astrodome, the Oilers had captured the spirit of working class Houston. At the Dolphins Monday Night Game, blue and white pom-poms were given out, and two locally produced fight songs, "Luv ya Blue!" and "Houston Oilers #1' were played routinely.

When the team arrived back to Houston's Astrodome on the Sunday night after the loss to Pittsburgh, they got off the bus to find the stadium filled with 55,000 people waiting to celebrate their accomplishments. A veritable parade had followed the team from the airport back to the Astrodome.

The Oilers improved to 11-5 the following year but still finished second to the Steelers. Campbell started the year with a 32-carry, 166-yard, 2-touchdown performance against the Redskins. He had 11 games of at least 100 yards rushing including seven in a row at the end of the season. The best of those was a 33-carry, 195-yard effort as the Oilers beat the Cowboys 30-24 on Thanksgiving Day on national television. He added 109 yards in a 20-17 win over the Steelers on Monday Night Football. He won MVP honors again with 1,697 yards rushing and 19 scores.

A better record meant the Orioles got to host a wildcard game, and they beat the Broncos 13-7. Campbell had the go-ahead touchdown, but it came at a cost. He suffered a leg injury that would keep him out of the next game. Also injured were quarterback Pastorini and wide receiver Kenny Burroughs. The Oilers were down to second string at their three most important offensive skill positions going into a road game against the high-powered offense of the San Diego Chargers.

In sunny San Diego, the Chargers were an 8-point favorite after going 12-4 and putting up 30+ points six times. Quarterback Dan Fouts had thrown for 4,082 yards and 24 touchdowns. The Oilers signed street free agent Boobie Clark to get some semblance of Campbell's power game, while quarterback

Gifford Nielsen, a BYU grad, got the start under center. But the real star of the game was a tall, muscular defensive back rookie from Jackson State named Vernon Perry. Perry had started all 16 games at strong safety for the Oilers and made three interceptions during the regular season. Against Fouts, he was otherworldly, intercepting four passes and blocking a field goal as the Oilers' defense rose to the occasion. Fouts threw five interceptions on the day and the Chargers' ground game was nonexistent.\

Meanwhile Clark, Rob Carpenter, and Tim Wilson combined to do their best Earl Campbell impersonation, carrying the ball 35 times for 136 yards and a touchdown. In the third quarter, Nielsen found receiver Mike Renfro on a 47-yard touchdown to give Houston a 17-14 lead and they never relinquished it, pulling the massive upset.

Perry continued his amazing streak the next week against the Steelers, returning an interception 75 yards for a touchdown to start the game. Down 17-10, the Oilers appeared to tie the game on a touchdown grab by Mike Renfro, but it was ruled out of bounds and Houston settled for a field goal. The Steelers went on to win 27-13. Still injured, Campbell managed just 15 yards on 17 carries. When the Oilers arrived back in Houston that night, they found 60,000 fans waiting them in the Astrodome. Bum Phillips took a microphone and told them, "Two years ago we knocked on the door, this year we banged on it, and next year we're going to kick the son of a bitch in."

At that moment, Philips could have won the governorship of Texas if he was so inclined. Campbell was at his very best in 1980, even if the Oilers had traded quarterbacks and installed Kenny Stabler. Campbell ran for more than 200 yards in four different games, a record that has never been broken. He finished the year with 1,934 yards, the second-most ever at the time, and scored 13 touchdowns to win a third straight MVP award. The Oilers tied Cleveland for the AFC Central title but lost it on a tie-breaker. They were upset by the Oakland Raiders in the wildcard round, and the window closed on them. They wouldn't make it back to the playoffs for seven years. Campbell added 1,376 yards in 1981. In four years, he had amassed 6,457 yards, the most ever by a player in his first four seasons.

FACTS AND FIGURES

1. In their 1966 56-7 win over the Philadelphia Eagles, the Dallas Cowboys amassed 32 first downs and 652 yards of total offense. Don Meredith completed 19 of 26 passes for 394 yards and five touchdowns. His rating for the game was 154.6. Bullet Bob Hayes caught six passes for 107 yards, three for touchdowns.

2. In 1973, the Cowboys had four rushers above 4.2 yards per carry, including quarterback Roger Staubach who averaged 5.4 yards on the ground and scored three touchdowns.

3. Tony Dorsett's rookie record of 1,007 yards rushing in 1977 was a Cowboys standard until 2016.

4. In Miami's perfect season of 1972, the Dolphins won seven games by 8 points or fewer.

5. The Dolphins won 15 straight from 1972-1973. After a loss to Oakland, they won 10 more games in a row.

6. The 1977 Steelers had eight of their starters on defense voted to the Pro Bowl.

7. Chuck Noll's career record with Pittsburgh was 209-156-1.

8. John Madden's two sons both played college football in the Ivy League—one at Brown and the other at Harvard.

9. Madden left Oakland with a career record of 103-32-7. His "worst" record was 9-7.

10. The 1984 San Francisco 49ers scored 252 points more than they allowed opponents.

11. The 1985 Chicago Bears outscored their postseason opponents 97-10.

12. William "The Refrigerator" Perry became the first lineman to score an offensive touchdown in Super Bowl history.

13. Only three teams have gone 18-1 in NFL history—the 1984 49ers, the 1985 Bears, and the 2007 New England Patriots.

14. Earl Campbell had eleven 100-yard rushing games in 1979, including seven straight.

15. In 1980, Earl Campbell had four games with at least 200 yards rushing.

TRIVIA QUESTIONS

1. Who dropped a certain touchdown catch for the Cowboys in the 1979 Super Bowl?

   A. Jackie Smith
   B. Drew Pearson
   C. Preston Pearson
   D. Tony Dorsett

2. Who was Miami's last opponent in its 14-0 regular season of 1972?

   A. Houston
   B. San Diego
   C. Minnesota
   D. Baltimore

3. For how many years did Chuck Noll coach the Steelers?

   A. 10
   B. 15
   C. 20
   D. 23

4. How many points did the Washington Redskins score in the second quarterback against Denver?

   A. 10

B. 20

C. 35

D. 40

5. Who was the only team to beat the 1984 San Francisco 49ers?

A. Atlanta

B. Tampa Bay

C. Washington

D. Pittsburgh

Answers

1. A
2. D
3. D
4. C
5. D

CHAPTER 5

THE MODERN NFL (1990-)

Expansion and Relocations

The NFL has been a changing place in the last twenty-five years, with teams moving cities and new teams coming on the scene. It started in the 1980s, when the Raiders moved to Los Angeles and the Colts left Baltimore for Indianapolis, that move coming in the dead of night. Colts owner Robert Irsay executed it on March 29, 1984.

Indianapolis had built the Hoosier Dome in an effort to attract a team. In early March, 1984, NFL owners gave Irsay the chance to move to either Phoenix or Indianapolis after Baltimore reused to spend $15 million on upgrading its own stadium. The mayor of Indianapolis offered the Colts a $12.5 million loan, a $4 million training complex, and the use of a new $77.5 million stadium. Working fast using Mayflower trucks, the team moved overnight to Indianapolis, an 8-hour drive away. The next day, the Maryland House of Delegates enacted a bill to seize the Colts as eminent domain, but it was too late. The trucks took different routes to avoid state police in Maryland and were escorted to the new facility by the Indiana State Police. Hall of Fame quarterback Johnny Unitas cut all ties with the organization after its move.

In 1996, the Cleveland Browns moved to Baltimore and became the Ravens. Unitas approached the Ravens and became an ambassador, and a statue of him is outside M&T Bank Stadium.

In the late 1980s, the struggling St. Louis cardinals moved to Phoenix. They called themselves the Phoenix Cardinals for five years before rebranding as the Arizona Cardinals in 1994.

In 1995, the league saw four moves as the Raiders moved back to Oakland, the Rams moved to St. Louis, and the Carolina Panthers and Jacksonville Jaguars came into existence.

The Browns became the Ravens the following year, putting Art Modell right up there with Satan when it came to hatred from Browns fans. Subsequent legal action allowed the city of Cleveland to maintain the Browns color, history, and records when the team got an expansion franchise in 1999.

In 1997, Bud Adams announced the Houston Oilers would move to Tennessee and become the Titans. Without a stadium ready, they played in Memphis in 1997 and at Vanderbilt Stadium in 1998 before moving to their new home as the Titans.

Houston was back in the game six years later with the Houston Texans playing at the stadium Bud Adams had so desperately wanted.

The league stayed static for the next fourteen years until 2016, when the St. Louis Rams moved back to Los Angeles after 21 seasons. A year later, LA got downright crowded when the Chargers announced they would be moving there as well.

A few weeks later, the Oakland Raiders announced they were moving to Las Vegas for the 2019 season.

The Herschel Walker Trade

Minnesota wanted a running back—really badly. Jerry Jones and Jimmy Johnson decided to see how badly. Johnson contacted Viking GM Mike Lynn to tell him they were about to trade Herschel Walker to the Cleveland Browns, and if the Vikes wanted him, they needed to put up an offer. Feeling they were close to a Super Bowl run, the Vikings agreed and received the Heisman Trophy running back along with four future Cowboy picks—none better than the third round. The Cowboys got five players in return, but more importantly nine draft picks. Yes, nine.

The first draft pick they turned into Emmitt Smith. Then came James Williams, Alvin Harper, and Darren Woodson. They traded other picks to get Russell Maryland. Those players formed the foundation that led to the Cowboys reemergence in the early 1990s. They won the Super Bowl in 1992, 1993, and 1995, with Smith pairing with Troy Aikman and Michael Irvin as one of the most powerful trios in NFL history. Smith became the NFL's all-time leading rusher, finishing with eight Pro Bowl appearances, 18,355 yards, and 164 rushing touchdowns. He was MVP of Super Bowl XXVIII and led the league in rushing four times. Walker was amazing to start, with 148 yards on 18 carries in a season-opening win over Green Bay, but the passion seemed to be missing. He played just 2-3 seasons for the Vikings and never totaled 100 yards in a season.

Greatest Show on Turf

Kurt Warner was two things before he was the quarterback of the St. Louis Rams, a grocery store sacker and the quarterback of an Arena Football League team. The Rams had been in St. Louis for five seasons by the time 1999 rolled around, and had yet to register a pulse, never finishing higher than third, and never making it above .500. Dick Vermeil was in his third year as head coach in 1999 and had signed Marshall Faulk as the team's new star on offense. He was supposed to team with Trent Green to run a sophisticated offense designed by coordinator Mike Martz, but Green tore his ACL in the preseason. With few options, Vermeil named Warner the starter. In a season opening win over Baltimore, Warner threw for 309 yards and three touchdowns. After the Rams' bye, he lit up the Falcons for 275 yards and 3 touchdowns, as Faulk had 172 yards total offense and a touchdown. In the team's' first true test, he torched the 49ers for 323 yards and five touchdowns, with Bruce catching four of those and racking up 134 yards.

Sports Illustrated featured Warner on the cover with the question "Who is this Guy?" Quite frankly even the Rams barely knew what to make of it. By season's end, Warner had thrown for 4,353 yards and 41 touchdowns. He had at least one touchdown in every game. St. Louis went 13-3 and was the top seed in the NFC playoffs. Warner put all doubts of his ability to rest in a wild 49-37 win over Minnesota in the divisional playoffs. He threw for 391 yards and 5 touchdowns. The Tampa Bay Bucs were a much sterner test, with their amazing defense holding the Rams largely in check. With 4:44 to play in the game, Warner finally found Ricky Proehl for the only score of the game and an 11-6 win to get St. Louis to the Super Bowl. There, they outlasted the Tennessee Titans 23-16, with Bruce catching a 73-yard touchdown pass to win the game with 1:54 to play. Warner signed a 7-year, $47 million contract after the season.

The Rams fell back to 10-6 in 2000 as Warner broke his hand and missed five games, during which the team went 2-3. Faulk was a vision, rushing for 1,359 yards and catching passes for 830 more, piling up26 touchdowns.

Warner was back to form in 2001, with 4,830 yards passing and 36 touchdowns. The team went 14-2, losing by three to the Saints and by seven to the Bucs. Faulk broke 2,100 yards total offense again and accounted for 21 touchdowns. Torry Holt became the go-to receiver with 1,363 yards, and Bruce added 1,106 more. In their wildcard opener, the Rams crushed Green

Bay 45-17 as the defense worked over Brett Favre, who threw six interceptions, three of which were returned for touchdowns, two by Aeneas Williams. Warner practically had the day off, throwing just 30 passes for 216 yards and two scores. The next week brought a thriller against the Eagles, with the Rams emerging a 29-24 victor, setting them up against the New England Patriots in the Super Bowl. Warner threw for 365 yards but only one touchdown, and was intercepted twice, suffering three sacks. A scrappy rookie named Tom Brady got the Patriots into position for a game-winning 48-yard field goal that marked the end of the Rams' reign.

Tom and Bill

Tom Brady was skinny and unimpressive at the NFL combine, which is why he was picked in the sixth round by the New England Patriots. Bill Belichick had been head coach of the Cleveland Browns for five years, going 36-44. Neither was much to think about when they joined the Patriots in 2000. In the seventeen years since, the two have become the most powerful and winning combination of head coach and quarterback of all time. They have combined to win five Super Bowls, appear in two others, and bring 14 AFC East titles home, including eight in a row heading into the 2017 season. Brady is the only player to win five Super Bowls for one team, and is the only four-time Super Bowl MVP. He enters the 2017 season fourth in career passing yards, fourth in career passing touchdowns, and third in career passer rating. He's never had a losing season as a starting quarterback, and his record in the postseason is 25-9. He's also married to supermodel Gisele Bundchen, just to rub salt in your wounds. He was the 199th pick in the draft in 2000. With three more strong seasons, he will become the NFL's all-time leader in passing yardage. He currently has 61,582 yards, although he is not the active leader, trailing Drew Brees' 66,111. Peyton Manning is first with 71,940 and Brett Favre second with 71,838.

Manning leads with 539 touchdowns, followed by Favre's 508. Brees is third with 465 and Brady fourth with 456. In seventeen years with the Patriots, Belichick has a record of 201-71, a winning percentage of 73.9%. His playoff winning percentage is 73.5%.

All Saints Day

On August 29, 2005, the city of New Orleans took massive damage from Hurricane Katrina. The Superdome, home of the New Orleans Saints, was unplayable, and more than 1,200 people lost their lives, with $108 billion in damages. The Saints, often the face of the city, never played a real home game in 2005, splitting games between San Antonio's Alamodome and Baton Rouge Tiger Stadium. There were no home games in New Orleans for 21 months until September of 2006. The game sold out in a heartbeat and was considered a defining moment in the city, and not just for the football team. The Falcons were set to punt on their first series when Steve Gleason broke through the line and blocked the punt, recovered for a touchdown by a teammate. The TV announcers wisely stayed quiet as the Superdome roared for more than a minute at the return of their beloved team, nearly a year to the day after the hurricane had nearly destroyed it. The Saints won that game and went on to their best season ever, finishing 10-6 before losing to the Chicago Bears in the NFC title game.

Three years later, they went 13-3 and won the Super Bowl. In July 2012, a statue of Gleason blocking the punt was placed outside the Superdome and was titled "Rebirth." Many believe that player sparked the season that likely saved the Saints from relocation. In April 2009, the team signed a deal to remain in New Orleans until at least 2025. In 2011, Gleason revealed he had developed Lou Gehrig's Disease (ALS). He continues to battle the disease to this day.

September 23, 2011

The attacks of September 11 on the United States postponed the following week's NFL schedule to January. Play did not resume until September 23, with a full slate of games, including the Washington Redskins playing at home on Monday night, the first sporting event since the attack on the Pentagon. NFL games had not been moved en mass since the attack on Pearl Harbor in 1941. At Dallas' Texas Stadium, Roy Williams burst from the tunnel carrying a huge American flag to the roars of tens of thousands.

At Soldier Field, a huge banner read "Chicago Loves New York, God Bless America." In San Diego, All-Pro linebacker Junior Seau wept openly during the national anthem. In Philadelphia, every Eagle carried a flag during the national anthem. The Bears covered the entire field with an enormous flag. The Lions and the Browns brought out a flag together. For one NFL player, it was simply too much. Arizona Cardinals' special teams player Pat Tillman retired and joined the US Army in 2002. He was the first football player killed in action since the Vietnam War.

Favre and Rodgers, Rodgers and Favre

Has a team ever been blessed at one position for so long? Surely never more than the Green Bay Packers, who haven't had to worry about their quarterback spot since 1992, a healthy 25-year stretch.

From 1992-2007, the Packers were led by all-time great Brett Favre, who guided them to a Super Bowl win in 1996, a Super Bowl appearance in 1997, and 11 playoff appearances in all. Since 2008, Aaron Rodgers has been leading the ship, and in that time the Packers have won another Super Bowl, made the playoffs all but one year, and won five division titles. Favre was the second-round draft pick of the Atlanta Falcons in 1991. Proving that most NFL scouts have no idea what they're doing, the Seahawks took Dan McGwire ahead of him, the Raiders Todd Marinovich. The Falcons let Favre threw four passes before trading him to Green Bay, where he started 253 out of 255 games over the next 16 years, going 160-93. He led the league in touchdowns four times, topping out at 39 in 1996, and lead in yardage twice, hitting for 4,413 years in 1995. He would not leave games while hurt, would not miss starts, and his worst record came in 2005 when the team went 4-12. They had a winning record every other season of his career.

His final year at age 38, he threw for 4,155 yards and 28 touchdowns. A free agent, he was cut by the Packers who were ready to install Rodgers in the role. He played three more years, taking the Vikings to the NFC title game in 2009, a postseason that included a win over the Packers.

Rodgers was the Packers #1 pick in the 2005 draft but did not throw more than 28 passes in a season until he became the starter in 2008, throwing for 4,038 yards and 28 touchdowns. He improved dramatically over the next few years, and in 2011 guided Green Bay to the Super Bowl, as he threw for 4,643 yards and 45 touchdowns against just six interceptions. Since 2009, he has only thrown double-digit interceptions once in a season, including tossing 40 touchdowns against seven picks in the 2016 seasons. Like his predecessor, Rodgers has been incredibly healthy, missing just nine games in nine years. His career record is 90-45, a winning percentage of 67%.

Peyton's Place

The Colts almost blew it and took Ryan Leaf. At the last minute, they remembered about Mr. Reliable. That's Peyton Manning if you're playing along at home. The Tennessee grad was the #1 pick for the Colts, starting every single game from his rookie season of 1998 until the end of 2010, when he missed the whole year with a neck injury. Despite a 3-13 first year, Manning's ability was never in question. He led the league in touchdown four times, breaking Dan Marino's record of 48 with 49 in the 2004 season, then shattering the mark at age 37, throwing 55 as a member of the Denver Broncos. He started 208 straight games and won 141 of them, throwing 399 touchdowns. Starting in 1999, he threw for more than 4,000 yards in every season but one. He led the Colts to the 2006 title and was named Super Bowl MVP.

In late 2010, he suffered an injury in the playoffs that required he miss all of 2011. The Colts went 3-13 and used their No. 1 draft pick on Stanford's Andrew Luck, a clear indication that Manning's days were over. He left for Denver and proved his career far from over, taking the Broncos to the 2013 Super Bowl and again in 2015, where he ended his career with a championship.

His longevity and consistency have Manning #1 in multiple NFL categories including:

Yardage (71,940) and touchdowns (539). While contemporary Tom Brady will likely go down as the greatest quarterback of all time, Manning was by far the most spectacular on any given Sunday.

Giant Undertaking

In 2007, the New England Patriots became the first team to ever go 16-0 in the regular season. They beat the New York Giants 38-35 to get to 16 wins. They entered the Super Bowl against those same Giants as a 12-point favorite after beating Jacksonville 31-20 and San Diego 21-12. Meanwhile, the Titans were a wildcard team and had to win three games on the road, doing so with wins at Tampa Bay (24-14), Dallas (21-17), and Green Bay (23-20 in overtime).

But what the Patriots hadn't planned on was the resilience of New York's offensive and defensive lines. The Giants controlled the clock throughout the game, with only 10 points scored in the first three quarters. It looked like New England would escape with the win when Randy Moss made a 6-yard touchdown grab with 2:42 to play to put the Patriots ahead 14-10.

New York started on its own 17-yard line with 2:39 to play and was rewarded with one of the greatest catches in NFL history as David Tree made a one-handed catch by pinning the ball to the crown of his helmet to gain 32 yards. With 35 seconds to play, Plaxico Burress caught a 13-yard touchdown pass from Eli Manning to give the Giants the 17-14 victory. Manning won the

Super Bowl one year after brother Peyton had done likewise with the Colts. Eli would add a second title when the Giants beat the Patriots again in 2012.

The Super Bowl Comeback

It was 21-3 at halftime during the 2017 Super Bowl as the Atlanta Falcons exerted their will on the New England Patriots, getting an 82-yard interception against suddenly mortal Tom Brady to go up 21-0. By the time New England scored a touchdown, it was 28-9, and Atlanta fans were gearing up for the biggest party the South had ever seen. The extra point was no good, and the onside kick failed. The Patriots got the ball back early in the fourth quarter and managed to get to the Atlanta 10 yard line before Brady was sacked. A short field goal made it 28-12 with 9:44 to play. The Falcons ran the ball as they had all game, but on 3rd and 1 with 8:31 to play, they tried to get cute and throw a pass. Instead, Matt Ryan was sacked and fumbled, and New England took over at the Falcon 25 with 8:24 to play, trailing by 16. The odds were still ever so long for every single person in the world not named Tom Brady. Unfortunately for the Falcons, Tom Brady was right across the line of scrimmage from them.

After a sack, he completed four straight passes, the last a 6-yarder to Danny Amendola, to make it 28-18. James White ran up the middle for the two-point conversion, and Atlanta's huge lead was now 28-20. The Falcons saw the Patriots stacking the box and threw the ball brilliantly for 39 yards to Devonta Freeman and 27 yards to Julio Jones, down to the New England 22 with 3:56 to play. A field goal would make it impossible for even Brady to come back. And yet on a second down play, the Falcons decided to throw the ball, and Ryan was dropped for a 12-yard loss. The 39-yard field goal attempt was now 52. The Patriots smartly took a timeout. Ryan threw a short pass for 9 yards on the next play when a run made infinitely more sense. A holding call against the Falcons pushed the ball back to the New England 45-yard line. Now the field goal would be 62 yards, foolish to even think about. Incredibly, the Falcons threw again as the clock stopped. It was well short of the first down, and they punted the ball back to Brady at his own 9-yard line with 3:30 to play.

Knowing full well the Patriots wouldn't dream of running the ball, the Falcons still couldn't stop them. Brady needed only one third-down conversion to move from his own 9 to the Atlanta 1, where White scored with 57 seconds to play to make it 28-26. Cool as a cucumber, Brady flicked a 3-yard out to Danny Amendola to tie the game at 28 with 52 seconds to play. Atlanta managed one first down and then had to punt, sending the game to overtime.

The Patriots had the ball first in the extra session and didn't even need a third-down conversion this time. They went for

5-for-5 to get to the Atlanta 25, and White moved the ball to the 15. A defensive pass interference penalty moved the ball to the two, and White trotted into the end zone to complete the greatest comeback in Super Bowl history.

FACTS AND FIGURES

1. The Carolina Panthers and Jacksonville Jaguars both made it to their respective conference championship games in their second years of play.

2. The Chargers went 56 years in San Diego before moving back to Los Angeles.

3. In 2000, the NFL realigned to eight four-team divisions.

4. The 2000 St. Louis Rams finished first in scoring and last in scoring allowed.

5. Tom Brady was just 16-of-27 for 145 yards in the Patriots' first Super Bowl win.

6. The games postponed following 9/11 were the first moved during the regular season since 1941.

7. Pat Tillman was the first NFL player to die in a war since Bob Kalsu in Vietnam in 1970.

8. Brett Favre and Aaron Rodgers combined to start 97% of the Packers' games at quarterback since 1992.

9. Peyton Manning is one of three pro quarterbacks from his family, along with brother Eli and father Archie.

10. T-shirts printed for the New England Patriots 19-0 season

that didn't happen were distributed to charities around the world.

11. The Giants used up 9 minutes and 59 seconds of clock in their opening drive against the Patriots in Super Bowl XLII.

12. James White had 14 catches for 110 yards in the 2017 Super Bowl, career highs in both categories.

13. Tom Brady set three Super Bowl records in 2017, most attempts (62), most completions (43), and most yards (466).

14. In 2017, there will be two teams playing in Los Angeles for the first time since 1994.

15. In 2008, the Detroit Lions became the only team to ever go 0-16 in a season.

TRIVIA QUESTIONS

1. Who did Kurt Warner replace at quarterback for the 1999 St. Louis Rams?

   A. Vince Ferragamo

   B. Jim Everett

   C. Trent Green

   D. Marc Bulger

2. What round did Tom Brady go in at the 2000 NFL draft?

   A. First

   B. Second

   C. Third

   D. Sixth

3. How many people watched the Super Bowl in 2008 on TV in the US?

   A. 50 million

   B. 75 million

   C. 97 million

   D. 150 million

4. How many points did the Patriots trail by at most during the 2017 Super Bowl?

   A. 15

B. 18

C. 19

D. 26

5. How many Super Bowl MVP trophies has Tom Brady won?

    A. 1

    B. 2

    C. 3

    D. 4

Answers

1. C
2. D
3. C
4. C
5. D

DON'T FORGET YOUR
FREE BOOKS